T0288043

SEIZING POWER

SEIZING POWER

The Grab for Global Oil Wealth

Robert Slater

BLOOMBERG PRESS
An Imprint of
WILEY

Published by John Wiley & Sons, Inc., Hoboken, New Jersey.
Published simultaneously in Canada.

For general information on our other products and services or for technical support, please contact our Customer Care Department within the United States at (800) 762-2974, outside the United States at (317) 572-3993 or fax (317) 572-4002.

Wiley also publishes its books in a variety of electronic formats. Some content that appears in print may not be available in electronic books. For more information about Wiley products, visit our web site at www.wiley.com.

Library of Congress Cataloging-in-Publication Data:
Slater, Robert.
    Seizing power : the grab for global oil wealth / Robert Slater.
        p. cm.
    Includes index.
    ISBN 978-1-57660-247-8 (hardback)
    1. Petroleum reserves.   2. Petroleum industry and trade.   I. Title.
    HD9560.5.S553 2010
    338.2'7282—dc22

                                                                        2010015434

Printed in the United States of America
10 9 8 7 6 5 4 3 2

Timeline

1970 December	Oil price per barrel: $1.80.
1973 October	OPEC refuses to sell oil to countries that support Israel in the Yom Kippur War. Oil price per barrel: $4.
1974 December	Oil price per barrel: $12. Some nations enact driving speed limits to conserve oil.
1979 November	Islamic Revolution and Iranian hostage crisis begin. Oil price per barrel: $70.
1981 October	Saudis flood market with cheap oil, forcing unprecedented price cuts by OPEC members. Oil price per barrel: $35.
1990 August	Iraq invades Kuwait. Oil price per barrel: $24.
1997 November	OPEC increases production. Oil price per barrel: $18.
1999 January	Iraq increases oil production. Currency crisis depresses Asian economies. Oil price per barrel: $10.
2000 September	Global oil output fears and bad weather increase oil prices. Oil price per barrel: $30.
2004 September	World becomes concerned about war in Iraq. Oil Price per barrel: $53.

2005 August	Hurricane Katrina strikes Gulf of Mexico. Oil price per barrel: $65.
2006 July	Tensions over Iran increase. Oil price per barrel: $77.
2007 September	OPEC announces output increase that is less than estimates. U.S. oil stocks fall lower than estimates. Six pipelines in Mexico are attacked by leftist group. Oil price per barrel: $80.
2007 October	Rising political tensions in eastern Turkey give rise to fear of violence. U.S. dollar declines. Oil price per barrel: $90.
2008 January	Oil price per barrel $100.
2008 March	Oil price per barrel: $110.
2008 May	Oil price per barrel: $130.
2008 June	Oil price per barrel: $138.
2008 September	Oil price per barrel: $95
2008 December	Due to the weakened global economy and the inevitable drop in demand for oil, oil price per barrel drops to $33.87.
2009 August	As signs of economic recovery increase, oil demand climbs. Oil price per barrel reaches $70 a barrel.
2010 January	Oil prices continue to rise, hitting $80 per barrel early this month.

—U.S. Energy Information Association

To two people whose dedication and skill and care have been manifested thousands of times and in thousands of ways on my behalf: words do not come close to expressing my gratitude and affection for Professor Deborah Rund and Dr. Michael Shapira

CONTENTS

Acknowledgments

I have written mostly about recent events in the history of oil, but the oil story actually began millions of years ago when geological processes began creating the substance in the earth that has since become such a valuable commodity. Only as late as 1859 did humankind even possess the knowledge or technology to bring the oil out of the ground, and, even then, it took the world a surprisingly long time to realize the benefits that could be derived from it. Once they were understood, however, world industrialization took a giant leap forward.

It was in 2006, when the price of oil had doubled from its price of three years earlier, $35 per barrel, that I became fascinated with the story. I began to look beyond oil's meteoric rise in price and realized some of the other profound changes the oil industry had experienced. I decided to learn more about the impact of oil on economics, on global politics, and on the capital markets. I wanted to learn how vastly different and complicated the new oil order had become.

I wanted, in short, to know the answer to the question that everyone was asking in 2008: how had we gotten into this situation, where oil could cost as much as $135 a barrel and gasoline $4 a gallon? How could all the nations of the world, whether developed or undeveloped, poor or rich, let themselves be held hostage to whoever controlled what came out of the ground?

How had we suddenly reached the tipping point where alternative energy sources began to be attractive—not because they were "greener" than oil, but because they might be *cheaper* than oil would one day be?

What had changed? And why? And why at this point in history? And what were the global implications for all of us?

If the "end-to-oil" activists are right, then a day of reckoning is fast approaching. As the demand for oil grows exponentially, and the supply becomes ever more elusive, it would be surprising only if the situation did *not* lead to violence.

It all makes for quite a story, and I want to share it with you here. I would like also to thank the many people who spoke to me on the record and the many more who were willing to speak only off the record.

Those who spoke to me on the record include the following people, and I thank them here: Mordechai Abir, Roscoe Bartlett, Ian Bremmer, Ray Carbone, Duncan Clarke, Anne Corin, Phil Davey, Eric Dezenhall, Robert Ebel, Ron Gold, Marshall Goldman, Larry Goldstein, Sharif Ghalib, Fadel Gheit, Charles G. Gurdon, Antoine Halff, James Hart, Alan S. Hegburg, Michael Hiley, Walter Kansteiner, David Knapp, Jim Kunstler, Doug Leggate, Michael Makovsky, Gerritt T. Maureau, Dan Miner, Edward Morse, Hugo Munro, Philip Nelson, Peter Odell, George Orwel, Lou Pugliaresi, John Rigby, Mike Robinson, Stephen Schlein, Michael D. Sherman, Fred Singer, Uisdean R. Vass, Lew Watts, Thomas E. Wallin, Mary Warne, Sarah Yizraeli, and Jennifer Semensa.

Introduction:
The Parable of São Tomé

The people [of São Tomé] are very friendly and its quite safe to go out in the park at night or even sleep on the beaches. The jungle is full of fruits and the ocean is full of fish, so the people do not have to worry about running out of food. There are no dangerous animals like tigers, lions, deadly snakes or spiders in the jungle. The most dangerous one is probably the mosquito that can give you malaria if you don't protect yourself.
— São Tomé and Principe government fact sheet, 2008

São Tomé and Principe, where oil was discovered in 2003, are two small islands off the coast of western Africa. Their combined population is about 200,000 and per capita income is $390. The São Toméan government has been trying to raise funds for its own further exploration and production to avoid having a technology "partner" take too big a slice of the oil-production pie.

The way the government has chosen to raise funds is creative, if a bit unorthodox. It has been renting the country's telephone lines to porn operators, who rout telephone-sex calls through them to various points on the globe. The country also sells commemorative stamps of Marilyn Monroe.[1]

São Tomé and Principe is only one of the players in the "new oil game." So far, it is a fairly benign player, relative to others such as Russia, Chad, Iran, and Venezuela, who can arguably be called *petroaggressors*, but events

---

[1] BBC News, July 16, 2003.

xiii

in São Tomé and Principe are an appropriate parable for the chaos of petropolitics today.

One hundred fifty years ago, when oil was first discovered, there was a great quantity of oil, but little need for it. A century and a half later, there is a great need for it and an insufficient quantity. Oil was governed, in the intervening years, first by the Rockefellers, Carnegies, and men of their ilk; then by the "Seven Sisters" and the global big oil companies; and then by the Organization of the Petroleum Exporting Countries.

The common thread that ran through all these titans of the oil industry was that they were all businesspeople, singly or collectively. Except for a couple of world wars that increased demand, oil's first 150 years were a period of relative stability in the oil markets.

But the order and stability enjoyed in the oil world in those years is not likely to be seen again. From the twenty-first century forward, oil fields and oil exploration will likely be characterized by unpredictability, chaos, and diminished supply. The world's oil is in decline. It may last another fifty or one hundred years, but the world could run out of oil at some point in the next century or century and a half.

Centuries from now, historians will look back at this twilight in the earth's evolution when civilization was oil-dependent. They will view it as a time in which nation competed against nation for the ever-scarcer and increasingly expensive commodity until a viable new source of energy was created to take over the job of running the world's machinery and transportation and to control the world's climate.

Until the world finds another cost-efficient fuel to run the engines of industry in the developed and developing countries, it risks being at the mercy of tyrants, terrorists, and speculators.

CHAPTER 1

Edging Toward Violence and Chaos

Crude oil may rise to between $150 and $200 a barrel within two years as growth in supply fails to keep pace with increased demand from developing nations, Goldman Sachs Group Inc. analysts led by Arjun N. Murti said in a report. . . . "The possibility of $150–$200 per barrel seems increasingly likely over the next six to twenty-four months, though predicting the ultimate peak in oil prices as well as the remaining duration of the upcycle remains a major uncertainty," the Goldman analysts wrote in the report dated May 5.

—"Goldman's Murti Says Oil 'Likely' to Reach $150–$200"
Nesa Subrahmaniyan, Bloomberg, May 6, 2008

In 2008, the price of oil had risen so dramatically that it dominated the global conversation and the global media. The inexorable increase in the price of gas at the pump threatened to destabilize the global economy. Fuel prices were forcing the world to spend a disproportionate portion of its income not only on fuel but also on grain as alternative-energy products displaced foodstuff agriculture.

The solutions proposed so far—from "gas-tax holidays" to presidential requests to the Saudis to increase supply—have been only Band-Aids, not long-term solutions, and the proposed reasons for rising oil prices have been controversial: Was it the Arabs, acting as a greedy cartel? Was it the 2 billion Chinese and Indians whose burgeoning middle classes were placing unsustainable demands on scarce supplies?

Was it some sort of satanic lobbying on the part of big Western oil companies against alternative-energy programs? Was it Wall Street speculators? What would the inflated oil prices do to economies already nearly down for the count from the subprime credit crisis?

The West was slow to see the warning signs of the oil-price run-up. As late as September 2003, when prices were less than $25 a barrel, Americans rarely exhibited any interest in oil. The only screaming at the gas pump occurred during the brief but troubling 1973–74 Arab oil embargo, when prices quadrupled from $2–$3 a barrel at the end of 1972 to $12 by the end of 1974.

With the new millennium, the benign indifference that we as a society had felt about oil began to morph into a vague curiosity and then into fascination. Suddenly, there seemed to be even more of a "Wild West" feeling in the business of oil than there had been in America's wild-catting days after oil's first discovery. We wanted to solve the riddle of how we had gotten into this mess and learn why every tyrant or upstart in every far-flung corner of the globe was holding our energy-dependent lifestyle hostage. We thought that if we could determine why the price of oil was climbing so quickly, then we might be able to find a way to reverse the trend and go back to "the good old days" when oil was just *there* and we didn't have to think about it. This was the hope before the latest power shift brought a massive reallocation of global oil wealth and before a new and dangerous set of oil players had come into existence, creating new rules for geopolitics and setting us on a path toward chaos and violence. To understand how we got to this place, we need to look at where we've been.

Until the end of the nineteenth century, the main oil consumer was the United States, and the forces of supply and demand within the oil market maintained an equilibrium. In the nineteenth and early twentieth centuries, powerful forces, mainly the Seven Sisters, which included U.S. and European oil companies, ruled the game. But, as new oil discoveries were made, power began to shift to the developing nations' national oil companies (NOCs). The original members of OPEC (Organization of the Petroleum Exporting Countries) were themselves NOCs, but they were largely under the thumb of the

The Original Seven Sisters

1. Standard American Oil of New Jersey (later Exxon)
2. Royal Dutch Shell
3. British Anglo-Persian Oil Company (later British Petroleum)
4. Standard American Oil of New York (later Mobil)
5. Texaco America (later Texaco)
6. Standard American Oil of California (later Chevron)
7. Gulf Oil

Saudis, who tried to maintain stability in the oil world, and, with a few notable exceptions, had not historically been one of the new national oil companies that were using their natural resources as weapons of aggression—the petroaggressors.

Rise of the NOCs

In the beginning, it was largely the big oil companies that still controlled exploration and production, but the new oil states were eager to wrest control of their own oil industries from the hands of the major international oil companies and so began to see an opportunity for their independence.

The crucial turning point—the power shift—between the old oil world and the new oil order came in the early 1970s. The event was significant not so much in its financial impact as in its political impact. When the Saudis declared an oil embargo during the 1973–74 Yom Kippur War, it was the first time the world had faced oil shortages when oil was used as a political weapon.

In the 1980s and 1990s, a sleeping tiger and a sleeping elephant began to awaken. The economic engines of China and India, with their 1 billion–strong populations and desire to create their own middle classes, demanded oil to fuel their growth and fulfill their dreams of prosperity.

Gazprom Aims for $1 Trillion Club on $250 Oil

CEO Alexei Miller of Gazprom said oil will reach $250 a barrel "in the foreseeable future," about 85 percent more than the current price, adding that the market value of the Russian energy company will triple to $1 trillion as early as 2015.

Market capitalization of the top three energy companies by value

Most active crude-oil futures trading on the New York Mercantile Exchange

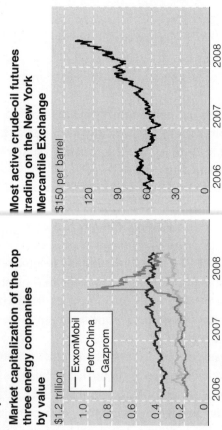

FIGURE 1-1 The diminishing supply of oil has led to a shifting cast of oil players—not only among the superpowers and the old "Big Oil" contenders, but also from the old players to the National Oil Companies (NOCs) in smaller, developing nations with highly unstable governments.

Source: Bloomberg.

6

It had been in the interest of the Saudis, the "alpha dogs" of OPEC, to keep the price sufficiently low so that consumers never felt pressure to seek alternative sources of energy. The Saudis sought to regulate oil prices by regulating the amount of oil they pumped. In the past, when prices had gotten too low, they pumped less; when prices became too high, they pumped more.

The system had worked fairly well. Westerners were loath to give up their oil addiction. Their established and luxurious lifestyles depended on it. But now there was a new dynamic as a result of the demand of the two emerging titans of Asia. India and China began to exert such a fierce pressure on oil supplies that the Saudis were finding it harder to keep oil prices low.

Third world rulers dreamed of finding oil the way they might have dreamed of winning the lottery: some to bring untold riches to their people, others simply to line their own pockets. The stage had been set for the next power shift—away from a stable and strong structure and toward the "anything goes" era of decentralization and the petroaggressors.

The rise of the NOCs, among them some of the most powerful oil enterprises in the world, was a key indicator that a new oil order now existed. Never even an issue before the early 1970s, the trend of higher oil prices seemed, by the early 2000s, to have taken on a frightening permanence. No feature of the new oil order had touched the immediate lives of so many people on a day-to-day basis as had rising oil prices.

The issue was not only about oil but also about what *kind* of oil, the most desirable being *light sweet* and the least desirable being *heavy sour*, with various other grades in between. The differences between grades related to the regions where they were produced and the technology and expense related to refining the different types and deriving useful distillate products.

THERE'S OIL, AND THEN THERE'S OIL

Crude oil comes in many varieties as categorized by sulfur content and viscosity. Oil that has a *high sulfur content* is referred to as "sour," while oil that has a *low sulfur content* is "sweet." Because sulfur is a pollutant, there are increasing "green" energy regulations that limit the use of distillates containing sulfur.

Viscosity relates to the density or thickness of the crude product (whether it's liquid or tarlike). Tarry crude oil is considered "heavy," and more liquid crude oil is "light."

Different distillates can generally be derived from each type of oil, but heavy sour requires a more expensive refining process, and many refiners are not set up to refine heavy sour. That means that the oil supply-and-demand picture is not only about one commodity but also about supply and demand for specific products and available refining capacity. Gasoline, for example, has higher U.S. demand in the summer months. Heating oil has higher demand during winter.[1]

Light Distillates Light distillates include propane, butane, naphtha, and gasoline. Light sweet crude, which is both very viscous and low in sulfur, is the single most popular segment, for which there is growing demand. (Europe, for example, is gradually switching to more efficient diesel vehicles.) Unfortunately, light sweet crude comprises only about one-fifth of global output. Its leading producers are the United States, United Kingdom (North Sea Brent), Nigeria, Iraq, and western Africa.

Heavy Distillates Heavy distillates include heating oil and shipping fuel. The leading producers of heavy sour crude are Saudi Arabia, Kuwait, Iran, Venezuela, Russia, and Mexico.

The New Petroaggressors

The changes that had begun in the oil world in the 1970s were subtle and often difficult to see at the time, but those changes were creating a power shift. Our exploration of the new oil order begins with two

---

[1] Platts energy information.

nations in Africa—Chad and São Tomé and Principe. For centuries, these had been resource-poor countries, but now in the twenty-first century, they were suddenly hoping to join the exclusive club of global oil producers. The irony and the potential for peaceful or violent rivalries were lost on no one.

CHAPTER 2

Two African Oil Nations: A Study in Contrasts

By the 1990s, oil was becoming more and more difficult to find, and yet environmental issues prevented the harvesting of oil in areas where geological prospects were highly favorable. The large, oil-producing countries were no longer averse to turning oil into a political weapon—nor were the small ones. Disorder reigned. In retrospect, relative to the fierce competition and violence in the oil industry in the twenty-first century, the twentieth century looked almost benign. . . .

Suddenly, every drop of oil counted. Now, tiny and previously little-heard-from nations were finding their way into the global spotlight. What lay at the root of the power shift was oil: who had it, who needed it. An interesting contrast can be made in seeing just how the discovery of oil was handled in two African nations— São Tomé and Principe and Chad.

São Tomé and Principe

From May until October, it does not rain in São Tomé and Principe, the tiny, two-island nation 150 miles off the coast of western Africa. For decades, the local people had fished, picked fruit from the jungle, and manufactured cacao for export. São Tomé and Principe might have looked like a veritable island paradise, but, in reality, the islands' citizens suffered in a yoke

For the decade up until 2005, the national budget of São Tomé and Principe had been averaging about $50 million a year, much of it from traditional crops like cacao. *Photo by Tom Cahill/Bloomberg News.*

of poverty that they seemed unable to cast off. Even the high price of cacao had little impact on their fortunes; in the early 2000s, they had suffered from a recent drought, and they had badly mismanaged their agricultural system.

São Tomé and Principe was the second-smallest country in Africa. It had no significant natural resources, and almost half its population was under the age of fourteen. One of the poorest countries in the world, it was a sleepy nation that had so far largely escaped the world's notice. In the past, the country had taken bailouts from Cuba, North Korea, and China just to survive. Like so many other tiny nations that were suddenly awakening to the modern world in the latter part of the twentieth century, São Tomé and Principe seemed to need a miracle.

In 2003, São Tomé and Principe's per-capita gross domestic product was estimated at $1,200. Its annual budget showed only $74.11 million in revenues. It was that rarest of nation-states, peaceful within, and peaceful without. Political scientists like to say that resource-poor countries are far less likely than rich ones to plant democratic roots, and that they inevitably breed violence, but the citizens of São Tomé and Principe proved the academics wrong.

Democracy did grow in São Tomé and Principe, beginning in 1991, but violence did not. Two coups—one in 1995, the other in 2003—failed. Politics became a ferocious, fast-paced series of shifting coalitions. There were fourteen changes of government in a twelve-year period— more even than in most other African countries.

Because São Tomé and Principe possessed negligible resources, the country's citizens lived without fear of outside aggression, but their economy seemed destined never to succeed. Most people lived in grinding poverty, many without running water or electricity. On June 19, 2004, in one of the scant references any newspaper made to the place, the British *Daily Telegraph* described São Tomé and Principe as a "run-down, fever-infested outpost of an old Portuguese empire with a history of slavery."

In 2005, 199,000 people had only 7,100 landline telephones, 12,000 cell phones, and 23,000 Internet connections. The country had only two hundred miles of roads, of which only ninety-nine miles were paved. It had only two airports with paved runways. Its one high school held classes in three five-hour shifts, and it had no university. For the decade until 2005, the national budget had been averaging about $50 million a year, much of it from traditional crops, such as coffee and cacao, or from fishing. Foreign aid amounted to

$35 million a year. Even by 2007, São Tomé and Principe's foreign exchange and gold reserves came to only $36 million; and its exports, about $4 million.

In the 1980s, as part of a deal with the Spanish government, São Tomé and Principe had agreed to accept Basque political prisoners from France. In exchange, São Tomé and Principe received a promise from France of an increase in foreign aid. In addition, the country had other, less orthodox ways to raise funds—phone-sex call routing and Marilyn Monroe postage stamps.

Like other national governments, the government of São Tomé and Principe felt compelled to maintain an army, even though its annual military budget was only $1 million. The bad news was that the army had no vehicles and no planes and was ill equipped to defend itself against enemies; the good news was that it had no enemies. When the United States announced that it was sending a military attaché to build up São Tomé and Principe's army, the citizens rejoiced despite the preposterousness of the mission and the lack of battle-ready soldiers. To the citizens of the tiny country, it must have seemed far too late for miracles, but a miracle came nevertheless.

In 1997, geological surveys revealed an enormous reserve of 4 billion to 11 billion barrels of oil just off the coast. The prospects were so good that a group of big oil companies offered São Tomé and Principe[1] $237 million for the right to look for offshore oil. Suddenly, the poor began to hope: oil not only could save them from poverty but also might even make them millionaires.

In 2001, President Fradique de Menezes, a former cacao merchant, took office. Early on, he vowed that, unlike Nigeria, his nation would not fall victim to the corruption that usually accompanied a reversal in a country's oil fortunes. The international community was delighted to find that not only did São Tomé and Principe's president speak of wanting to use the oil wealth to help his country but also that

---

[1] Less than half of the money ended up going to the country because Nigeria, having borne the initial cost of oil production, took in 60 percent. Nevertheless, São Tomé and Principe's portion was still four times the size of its 2004 government revenues.

the country looked more like a European state than an African one. The citizens' clothes, the country's architecture, the local cuisine, and the language (Portuguese) were all European. Ethnic conflict, instability, and government brutality were conspicuously absent. That's what the oil industry liked, and that's what many executives were counting on: ensuring political stability and the flow of oil profits to ordinary people.

When the exploration began in 2003 and when oil was actually discovered, wonder of wonders, it was all in São Tomé and Principe's territorial waters. The people had not dared hope for a miracle, but they had gotten one nevertheless. It wasn't that São Tomé and Principe's balance sheet couldn't do with an injection of good news— and a bit of cash—it was just that poor countries did not have such gifts land on their doorsteps; even if they did, the citizens of São Tomé and Principe had neither the technology nor the knowledge needed to make the raw material into a commercially viable commodity.

It was hard for the São Tomé and Principeans to take the discovery seriously, because the reality was that it would take time before anyone could successfully produce a single barrel of oil for export. It had only been in 2000–01 that São Tomé and Principe and Nigeria had hurriedly settled their disputed maritime border and agreed to jointly explore for oil in offshore waters. It had been predicted then that the Joint Development Zone could be producing 250,000 barrels of oil a day within five years. For a country to be counted as a genuine oil player, however, it had to produce a minimum 1 million barrels of oil a day. Even over time, said a few skeptics, there would be no "trickle-down" economics; most likely, any revenues would remain in the coffers of the politicians.

In 2004, ChevronTexaco, ExxonMobil, and the Norwegian firm Equity Energy shared the winning bid of $123 million for one of nine exploration blocks. The development race was on. Swedish firms began looking for telecommunications projects, Belgian enterprises sought work in construction, and companies from the United States, China, Norway, and Canada sent teams to the islands.

Why all the fuss about such a small producer? First, São Tomé and Principe offered the type of sweet crude that was easily refined into

Timeline for São Tomé and Principe

1997   Geological surveys suggest possibility of oil in São Tomé and Principe.

2000   August: Poorly defined maritime border with Nigeria is settled hurriedly in anticipation of oil exploration. Joint Development Zone is established by the two states.

2001   De Menezes is sworn in as president.

2002   De Menezes announces plans for a U.S. naval base in the country to protect São Tomé and Principe's oil interests.

2003   Oil is discovered.

2003   October: Oil companies bid for offshore oil blocks controlled by São Tomé and Principe and Nigeria. Bids are expected to generate hundreds of millions of dollars in license money for São Tomé.

2004   May: Economist Jeffrey Sachs meets with government officials in São Tomé, the nation's capital.

2004   December: Parliament approves oil law designed to protect revenues from corruption.

2005   February: São Tomé and Principe and Nigeria sign first offshore oil exploration and production-sharing agreement with international oil firms.

2006   Chevron, the operator of Block 1, announces that an oil discovery it has made will not be commercially exploitable.

2010   Oil production likely to begin.

lead-free gasoline. Second, São Tomé and Principe was not a member of OPEC and therefore had no obligatory production quotas, and its sizable offshore reserves could be loaded onto tankers without any foreign company setting foot on the country's soil. Finally, to oil-consuming nations, São Tomé represented a badly needed hedge against risks of oil-flow interruption elsewhere on the globe: If a bomb went off in Saudi Arabia, or a strike occurred in Venezuela, oil prices would inevitably soar. In that event, every drop of oil would count, and the 15 percent of American imports from western Africa would be indispensable. Because São Tomé and Principe held a strategic position in the oil-rich Gulf of Guinea, the United States announced that it would build a naval base in the gulf to monitor and guard the oil platforms and movements of oil tankers. Eager to allay any fears the island nation might have about foreign intervention in its politics, President George W. Bush assured de Menezes that the military would not base itself on the islands of São Tomé and Principe, but would stay on board ships off the coast. De Menezes applauded the step, because, for starters, the base would offer employment to local citizens, who were then facing an unemployment rate of 55 percent. That a country such as the United States was even interested in the tiny islands indicated how the oil world had changed.

As President de Menezes himself noted, after 9/11 the world needed alternative sources of oil outside the volatile Middle East. His country, he reminded interested parties, lay in a "strategic location in the world's most important oil region—in the deep sea of Africa's west coast." Although many people would have argued that the Middle East would still be the world's most important source for oil, no one could deny that western Africa was becoming increasingly important. Americans were already importing 15 percent of their oil from sub-Saharan Africa; that figure was expected to grow to 25 percent within a few years.

Now the citizens of São Tomé and Principe were taking their oil seriously—so seriously that they wanted to spend the oil revenues even before they got them. For a while, there was a feeling in the air of a boomtown in the making, and American lobbyists and oil-men visited the island. But old-timers in the oil business know that production does not quickly follow discovery, and the boom was made up more of the excitement about the prospect of oil than the oil itself.

President de Menezes, wanting to be sure his country used its newfound riches wisely, turned to Professor Jeffrey Sachs, of Columbia University in New York, an American expert on development aid who saw a chance to turn São Tomé and Principe into a model of how a poor country could handle oil successfully—neither engaging in violent conflicts nor becoming dependent on the commodity. As a result, in December 2004, São Tomé and Principe passed a new oil law that was the best of its kind in the world: it required that oil revenues be deposited directly with the Federal Reserve Bank of New York. Of those funds, only a small share could be absorbed into the local budget; the remainder had to be saved for the future. Control of the oil itself belonged to a commission made up of São Toméans.

Sachs continued to work with officials on issues of transparency, oil legislation, development, and malaria control, but, with oil production not expected for some time, the promise of the oil project diminished, and, "The boom was relatively short-lived. . . . Legislation was enacted, but whether it would stand up to the stresses of real oil flows remained to be seen. What we were trying to do was to create a framework so that, if oil came, it wouldn't be immediately squandered; it would lead to schools, roads, and clinics. . . . We were never sure if we could succeed, but I thought it was worth a try. . . . It's amazing how a population of 140,000 could have so much politics," says Sachs, shaking his head.[2] In 2009, drilling was finally under way and commercial production was expected in a few years.

Chad

Not far to the north of São Tomé and Principe lies Chad. Similar in many ways to São Tomé and Principe, Chad is a nation deep in the heart of Africa and mostly poor. In the 1960s, low-quality crude oil was discovered in Chad, but there was no great rush to install the infrastructure to pump it because investors feared political instability and corruption. The situation in Chad continued to be volatile for some thirty years.

---

[2] Jeffrey Sachs, interview with the author, April 29, 2008.

Activist Idriss Déby assumed the office of president on December 2, 1990, at the age of thirty-eight. A Muslim, he had been married several times and had at least a dozen children. Although he was only the son of a herder, he entered the Officers School in N'Djamena, the capital of Chad. He was sent to France after that; when he returned to Chad in 1976, he had his professional pilot certification. He was loyal to the army and to President Félix Malloum until the government fell apart in 1979.

Déby then tied his fortunes to those of Hissène Habré, a Chadian warlord. Habré became president in 1982; in exchange for his loyalty, Déby was made commander in chief of the army. He distinguished himself in 1984 by destroying pro-Libyan forces in eastern Chad. In 1985, Habré sent him to study at the Parisian École de Guerre. When he returned home, he was made Habré's chief military adviser. Nevertheless, in 1989, a rift developed between Habré and Déby over the increasing power of the presidential guard. When Habré accused Déby of preparing to mount a coup d'état, Déby fled to Libya and then to Sudan, where he formed the Patriotic Salvation Movement, an insurgent group supported by Libya and Sudan, which attacked Habré in Chad in October 1989. In early December 1990, Déby's troops marched, unopposed, into N'Djaména. He was elected president of Chad on February 28, 1991, with 64.67 percent of the vote.

THE CHADIAN ECONOMY IN THE 1980S

Chad gained its independence from France in 1960. It is a landlocked, semi-arid country, and, at that time, it was dependent on a single cash crop: cotton. In 1985, the World Bank ranked Chad as one of the five poorest nations in the world.

Chad's 1985 population of about 10 million had a per capita gross national product of just $160. Eighty percent of people lived on less than a dollar a day, and 98.5 percent of citizens had no electricity, potable water, or access to basic sanitation. Dung or wood was the principal cooking fuel.

World prices for cotton, Chad's single cash crop, had collapsed in 1985. Chad's second-largest source of income came from raising cattle, but one-third of its national herd of 4.7 million head was lost during the 1984–85 drought.

Douala, in Cameroon, the closest port to Chad's capital, is 1,056 miles away. By the mid-1980s, the only paved roads linking the capital to the interior had disappeared for lack of maintenance. Of the estimated 19,000 miles of dirt roads and tracks, only 780 miles were passable during the rainy season. Chad had no railroads, and its international airport had been destroyed by armed hostilities in 1980–81.

In 1985, the country had only two international telephone lines.

THE CHAD PIPELINE

Though oil had first been discovered in Chad in the late 1960s, thirty years of civil war in Chad provided a good reason for foreign investors to stay away.

In 1999, the international community decided to employ Chad as a test case for using oil revenues to lift the poor out of their predicament. At the initiation of a joint venture between the government of Chad and an ExxonMobil-led consortium of other oil-production companies, the World Bank laid out plans for a 650-mile-long pipeline that could handle 225,000 barrels a day. The pipeline would run all the way from Cameroon to the Gulf of Guinea and connect Chad's southern oil fields to terminals on the Atlantic coast of Cameroon, where the oil would be shipped to the West. The bank saw the arrangement as a brave new plan to reduce poverty, not only in Chad, but also in other similar resource-rich and developing nations. The country's oil-production plans were moving forward. With financing for the project in place, Chad soon became an attractive destination for international investment.

In exchange for its participation, the World Bank insisted on a legal condition—adherence to the Petroleum Revenue Management Law (PRML)—for backing a pipeline linking Chad to Cameroon's Atlantic coast. In accepting the condition, the government of Chad promised not to amend any provisions of the law in a way that would "materially and adversely affect" the poverty-reduction strategy of the PRML.

In case of a breach of contract by Chad, the World Bank could suspend new grants, halt disbursement of funds, and demand accelerated repayment of existing loans.

With the agreement in place, the bank kicked in $190 million to jump-start the project. With expectations of being completed in July 2003, the pipeline project had a dual purpose: it would not only bring Chadian oil to the outside world but also prove that oil could promote growth among underdeveloped nations.

Chad did not begin pumping oil until 2003. Although the annual output was a modest 250,000 barrels per day, investors, especially American giants Chevron and ExxonMobil, and the Malaysian national oil company, Petronas, were interested in Chad's fresh fields and uncharted parts of its desert. Hard as it may be to believe, by 2004, thanks to foreign investment and oil exported via the new pipeline, Chad had the fastest-growing economy in the world.

Déby *sounded* well intentioned. He insisted that Chad would use part of the pipeline income for the national welfare budget. Ten percent of government funds would be earmarked for road, health, water, and education infrastructure. The Chadian plan to set aside oil revenues for the poor was regarded as admirable, a breath of fresh air after corrupt politicians in other African oil-producing nations such as Nigeria, Congo-Brazzaville, Gabon, and Angola had no qualms about lining their own pockets with oil money. The oil-pipeline accord in Chad was regarded as an ideal way to aid third world nations in emerging from impoverishment and corruption. The industrialized world watched the Chad experiment with growing interest.

The pipeline at first seemed to bring little improvement to Chad's population. The traffic lights in N'Djaména were so dim as to be useless because Chad did not produce enough electricity and its generators did not work properly. Traffic, however, was not much of a problem because most of the country's gas stations stood abandoned. On dusty street corners in the heart of N'Djaména, bags of peanuts were being offered for sale by crowds of children who would, most likely, not live to age forty-five. With the average wage below a dollar a day, few Chadians could afford health care.

Outside ExxonMobil's offices, on the other hand, generator-powered security lights cast light that was bright enough to allow children to do their homework at night. The World Bank had insisted that oil money be earmarked for the poor, but the Chadian government appeared to have other priorities. The group of citizens who would decide how the oil money would be spent was filled with the president's close friends, and when Déby received the first oil payment from Exxon in 2004, he spent it on military hardware.

With oil companies starting to explore other parts of Chad in 2005 and 2006, forecasts of what Chad's oil profits would be in the near future were revised significantly upward. The first three oil fields in southern Chad, it was said, could bring in $5 billion in oil profits over the next twenty-five years, the fields' predicted production span.

Chad went only from the tenth- to the fourth-poorest nation in the world, but President Déby seemed far more concerned with his own safety than the welfare of his people: when he arrived in the capital, streets were emptied, stores looked up, and cars removed from sight. Orders were given that even someone seen peeking from a window would be shot. In 2005, while the pipeline project was generating $306 million, a watchdog group, Transparency International, ranked Chad as the most corrupt nation in the world.

Elections in Chad had been scheduled for May 3, 2006, but, on April 13, some 600 rebels stormed the capital, threatening the Déby government. Soon the streets of N'Djaména filled with pickup trucks full of men armed with rifles. Some of the men wore brown camouflage garments issued to the army; others preferred the gowns and turbans that residents of the capital routinely wore. These were Déby's forces, there to defend him against the Sudan-based Chadian rebels trying to depose him.

If Déby were going to succeed, he needed the World Bank to ease its rule on how Chad spent its oil money. The Chadian parliament took the extraordinary step of changing the PRML; it would now permit a $50 million payment of oil revenues from ExxonMobil to bypass the World Bank account earmarked for development projects and be transferred directly to the government. The legislative maneuver was a definitive act of defiance against the World Bank by a tiny nation, one of the new breed of petroaggressors. The World Bank responded by freezing a London escrow account of $125 million in Chadian oil royalties and cutting $124 million in further financial assistance.

Déby's reaction to the World Bank's freezing the funds was to close Chad's new pipeline unless and until the ExxonMobil-led consortium paid him $100 million. Meanwhile, Chad wanted to make sure its stream of oil revenues continued from its proven oil reserves of 1.5 billion barrels of oil. Although it lacked a refined infrastructure, Déby could rely on Cameroonian and Nigerian infrastructure for transport. As a show of bravado, Déby warned that he could find other investors friendlier to Chad than those in the consortium, particularly since the price of oil was continuing to rise. Of the $306 million Chad had received in oil revenues, only $27.4 million of it had already been put aside for development; future funds were soon diverted to purchase arms to keep Idriss Déby's government in power. The World Bank knew it could no longer trust Déby. His second and final five-year mandate was to have ended in May 2006, but he altered the constitution in 2004 to eliminate term limits.

The Chadian conflict with the World Bank had ended with a great victory for Déby. Paul Wolfowitz, the head of the World Bank, was so taken aback by Chad's audacity that he gave Déby all he asked for, resuming both loans and oil payments. The mouse had roared, and the lion had capitulated. But Chad was nevertheless eager for additional World Bank support, and so reached a compromise agreement with the World Bank in July 2006, agreeing to earmark 70 percent of its oil earnings to combat poverty. Then it promptly launched a spending spree on guns, aircraft, armored vehicles, and Humvees.

Although "small potatoes" by international standards, and with a high sulfur content that reduced their value, Chad's oil exports of 160,000 barrels a day might nevertheless make the difference between the World Bank's turning over the funds Déby had been demanding and not—at least that was what Déby hoped. The world's oil supply had been so diminished that even a country with oil as scant in quantity and as poor in quality as Chad's had leverage against an institution such as the World Bank.

In August 2006, Déby complained Chad had only been receiving what he called "crumbs" from foreign companies running the industry and called for his country's stake in its oil output to rise to 60 percent. In addition, he said Chevron and Petronas had refused to pay his government $486.2 million in taxes he had imposed on them.

All this machismo might have strengthened his political position at home, but, in the eyes of sophisticated oil watchers abroad, Déby was taking a big chance by putting at risk his relationships with precisely those institutions he needed the most to move his oil game forward.

As of late 2008, Chad remains a dictatorship, and Déby's ouster is only a matter of time. Chad calls itself a democracy, but, since gaining independence from France in 1960, its government has not changed hands peacefully even once.

Unlike São Tomé and Príncipe, Chad had learned to exploit its newfound oil to gain leverage; it had learned to tie international institutions up in knots and keep the largest oil companies in the world vying for position within its borders. Chad's maneuverings and manipulations over oil were one of the more poignant indications that small oil producers such as Chad could play the oil game well enough to gain the

You Know You're in Trouble When . . .

Chad's efforts at taking on the World Bank aroused the interest of more than a few in the West and prompted Jim Jubak, an MSN Money Web columnist, to note: "Boy, you know you're in trouble when Chad, a country of 8.1 million people living on 1.3 million square miles of desert, can push you around." There was no reason to feel sorry for the giant oil companies yet, but, increasingly, nations such as Russia, Iran, Venezuela—and even Chad—were calling the shots.

status of major oil players. It was a textbook case of a petroaggressor making inroads within the new oil order.

In the next chapter, we shall look at the growing relationship between China and Africa. If any two groups ever seemed like odd political bedfellows, it was the Chinese and Africans—but when they did get together, it had a great deal to do with oil.

CHAPTER 3

China Invades Africa

Ever since the 1973–74 Arab oil embargo, both Western and Asian nations have had reservations about being dependent on Middle Eastern oil. The United States, for one, although far from having a disengagement policy with the Gulf states, had been looking for a way to put an end to its "addiction" to Arab oil. The events of 9/11 had only exacerbated the world's fears. Alternative sources of energy not only would need to be "green," or good for the environment (and therefore also good politics), but also free the United States from certain aspects of dependency on oil-producing nations. Unfortunately, although alternative-energy concepts (for example, windmills, solar panels, ethanol) and energy-conservation measures (such as smaller cars and lower speed limits) were all valiant efforts, realistically the developed world should have embarked on such a path many years earlier. And now there were also developing economies, whose growth was like a hungry beast that demanded to be fed. A more immediate energy solution would have to be found. . . .

There had not been much good news out of Africa for a long time. Most of the world, when it thought of Africa, thought of civil wars, famines, the AIDS epidemic, high infant-mortality rates, massive poverty, and official corruption. The discovery of oil, however, offered hope for changing the lives of many Africans for the better.

A tremendous amount of economic and political power was now handed not only to São Tomé and Principe and Chad, which we discussed in Chapter 2, but also to Equatorial Guinea, Gabon, and several other tiny African states.

The big oil companies first went into Africa with the hope that the continent would provide them with new sources of oil. As time went on, though, Africa seemed to present as many new problems as it offered solutions to old ones. The companies found that doing business with the Saudis and Kuwaitis had been easy compared with doing business with the Africans. Middle Eastern countries, however unstable they might have appeared, at least had political regimes that might be counted on to last for a generation or so, whereas in Africa, coups sometimes occurred every few months. One might make a deal with a self-styled rebel general today—and find tomorrow that he had been summarily dispatched. Better, they reasoned, the devil one knew. Some of those early investors stayed on, but a few began to depart Africa, presenting opportunities for nations with less fear of uncertainty and less concern about the potential dangers of African unrest.

By the early 1990s, despite political problems and production interruptions, African oil was starting to make a dent in meeting the world's oil needs; forecasts of how many barrels of oil the Africans could pull from the ground were optimistic. Early predictions said that, by 2015, Africa's share of the U.S. oil market would grow from 15 percent to 25 percent. If that turned out to be accurate, then Africa might replace the Middle East as the dominant source of foreign oil for the United States in as little as eight years. Things certainly seemed headed in that direction. In 2001, American imports from the Middle East had surpassed African oil imports by little more than 10 percent, or 1.3 million barrels a day. The two major oil-producing areas were now more or less equivalent. Oil supplies from Africa and the Middle East each accounted for a 22 percent share of American crude-oil imports, but this equilibrium would begin to shift toward Africa over the next few years.

In 1982, China's economy was growing at an annual rate of 9 percent; in 1993, at 13 percent; and in 2006, at 11.3 percent. Chinese leaders had a quandary regarding their nation's growth rate. To guarantee their citizens' continued support for the existing political system, these leaders would have to offer at least the possibility of a middle-class life. But, in assessing how to supply their energy needs for that strategy, they were faced with a situation that was changing under their feet.

By 1989, oil supplies were growing tight, and new entrants on the demand side of the equation had to search outside the traditional channels. What remained was the smaller, more unstable, and often more dangerous states—many of them in Africa. Experts were forecasting that, by 2045, China would depend on imported oil for 45 percent of its oil needs. There was no longer any doubt: if China was to address its domestic-growth agenda and become a net importer of oil, then Africa would be critical to its plan.

China had discovered oil in 1959, elevating it to the status of a potential player in the oil markets, but its own oil fields would never be able to keep pace with the rapidly expanding economy. Finally, in 1993, the balance of China's domestic oil supply and its economy's growth rate changed the balance: China became a net importer of oil. Throughout the 1990s and early 2000s, it was oil that brought the nation of China and the continent of Africa together. China was eager to fuel its economic growth engine, and Africa lacked the knowledge and technology to convert its newly discovered resource from raw commodity to revenue. The timing was perfect for both. That the Chinese might also not be so likely to fuss about certain other issues the West seemed concerned about—such as bribery, corruption, and human-rights offenses—just made it that much easier for the Africans to do business with the Chinese. As oil prices began to soar, the Africans had other suitors as well—such giants as Total, Elf, and Royal Dutch Shell, ExxonMobil, and ChevronTexaco— but the Chinese demand for oil was becoming particularly voracious: beginning in 2004, it accounted for 40 percent of the entire growth in global oil demand, already surpassing Japan, and was now second only in oil consumption to the United States. Oil experts termed western Africa the new El Dorado of the oil industry. Some analysts believed that the region held 10 percent of the world's reserves. The United States was said to have imported more oil from western Africa than from the Middle East in 2005. Nigeria, the oil giant of the African region, was supplying 10 to 12 percent of American oil imports.

By 2006, the entire oil picture had changed from a decade earlier: American oil imports from Africa had surpassed those from the

Middle East, and Chinese trade with Africa had soared to a monumental $55 billion. The forging of Chinese–African partnerships was key to the new oil order. Oil was indeed making strange bedfellows.

The Chinese invaded Africa, not with guns, but with money and influence. In 2005, Chinese companies invested $175 million in Africa in oil-exploration projects and infrastructure, road and railway construction, and agricultural programs and education. On January 10, 2006, the state-owned Chinese oil company CNOOC announced that it planned to purchase a 45 percent stake ($2.27 billion) in an offshore oil field in Nigeria, and the Chinese were buying 64 percent of Sudan's oil exports.

By early 2007, the Chinese were continuing to seek oil—not only in the Sudan, Nigeria, and Chad, but also in Angola, Algeria, Gabon, Equatorial Guinea, and the Republic of the Congo. The Chinese approach to drilling oil in Africa appealed very much to the Africans. Whereas Canada and the United States seemed to care only for the big finds, the Chinese were pleased to get their hands on even the small finds, taking the position that diversity had its advantages in a continent as unstable as Africa.

Through China's investments and appetite for raw materials, the world's most populous country was transforming economies from Angola to Australia. But what was also significant was that China was turning its new commercial might into political muscle, striding onto the global stage and acting like a nation that very much intended to become the world's next great power.

THROUGH PROSPERITY, DOMINANCE

The conventional wisdom was that the Chinese were concerned with more than their domestic growth. No Chinese government leader would admit to it, but the Chinese exhibited all the signs that they wanted to dominant the globe in the twenty-first century.

For the Chinese, investing in Africa and elsewhere was one part of an overall political strategy, and oil was another part. Historically, most of Chinese foreign policy had consisted of vitriolic attacks on imperialism. China had seen the world as black and white: what was

Chen Yun, president of the China Development Bank, cuts a ribbon at the opening ceremony of the China-Africa Development Fund at the Great Hall of the People in Beijing, China, on Tuesday, June 27, 2007. China has promised US$20 billion in infrastructure and trade financing support to African nations over the next three years. *Photo by Shaver/Bloomberg News.*

good for the United States or the West would automatically be bad for China, and vice versa. Isolating themselves from the rest of the world, the Chinese had not considered it important to learn English[1] and had shown little enthusiasm for Western artistry or industry. Now they were realizing that interactions and transactions with the West could prove valuable and that diplomacy and foreign aid had some value in terms of influence. At international meetings, Chinese communiqués softened, and the old standard condemnations of the West were absent. Instead, the Chinese often lent the clout of their size and their voting power to the Africans.

"It used to be," said President Déby of Chad, "that when we had problems with our neighbor sending mercenaries to invade us, none of

---

[1] Many young Americans and Europeans, on the other hand, have been quite eagerly studying Mandarin Chinese!

our complaints before the United Nations would pass, because China blocked them." Since then, Angola had broken off relations with Taiwan to curry favor with Beijing and open the door to Chinese investment. Now, added Déby, "We have been able to raise our concerns without taboo."

The Chinese now looked less like bit players and more like major oil players in Africa. They had trained thousands of Africans in Chinese universities and sent thousands of physicians to Africa, acts that the Africans remembered. Hu made several promises: to double Chinese aid to Africa by 2009, to train fifteen thousand professionals, to provide scholarships to four thousand African students, and to aid the continent's agricultural programs.[2]

Hu: A Chinese Leader with Big Plans

Sixty-four-year-old Chinese president Hu Jintao has been a surprisingly ambitious leader. In the early 1960s, while still a student at university, he joined the Communist Party, and has been a loyal member ever since.

Although Hu seemed uncomfortable when meeting with foreigners, he nevertheless served as China's most important and most active ambassador beginning in 2004. He spent two weeks in South America that year, pledging billions of dollars in investments to Argentina, Brazil, Chile, and Cuba. He also spent time in Kenya, Nigeria, the United States, Russia, Saudi Arabia, and Morocco.

At the end of 2006, Hu had hosted forty-eight African national leaders for three weeks of talks in Beijing as a way to launch the Chinese "invasion" of Africa.

---

[2] Hu did not forget the rest of the world: in 2006, he traveled not only to Vietnam for the annual Asia-Pacific Economic Cooperation summit but also to Laos, India, and Pakistan.

Angola

Angola first discovered oil in 1955, but it would be years before anyone knew how substantial the nation's reserves actually were. As of January 2007, Angola's proven oil reserves were estimated at 8 billion barrels, the majority of which lay in blocks more than one hundred miles offshore. Angola's oil production increased tenfold from the mid-1970s to reach 1.4 million barrels a day in 2005 and 1.5 million barrels a day in 2006. Crude-oil production had more than quadrupled over two decades. According to Energy Information Administration (EIA) estimates, Angolan oil production was set to reach 2 million barrels by 2008 when new deepwater production sites were expected to come online. In December 2006, the World Bank announced that, consistent

Customers enter and leave a branch of Standard Bank in Rosebank, Johannesburg, South Africa, Oct. 25, 2007. Industrial & Commercial Bank of China Ltd. paid 36.7 billion rand ($5.6 billion) for a 20 percent stake in Standard Bank Group Ltd., Africa's largest bank, in the biggest overseas acquisition by a Chinese company. *Photo by Naashon Zalk/Bloomberg News.*

with EIA estimates, Angola's oil production would likely equal that of Kuwait by 2011: 2.6 million barrels per day.

Oil companies around the world had suspected that Angola might be one of the last large untapped regions to contain oil. In 2006, to secure rights to drill offshore, the Italian oil company Eni bid the extraordinary amount of $902 million. It was then the highest fee an oil company had ever paid for drilling rights.

"At that time it seemed crazy," said Paolo Scaroni, Eni's chief executive. "In reality we feel it was not crazy at all. There are big deposits in Angola. It's an area of Africa where production can only grow and we want to be part of that growth."[3]

After Eni's bid, Sinopec, a Chinese state-owned company, and Sonangol, an Angolan national oil company, jointly offered $2.2 billion for two other offshore blocks belonging to Angola.

In 2006, Angola ranked 142nd out of 163 countries in Transparency International's annual corruption-perception index. The International Monetary Fund (IMF) was reluctant to dole out any more money unless Angola adequately explained what happened to the $4 billion in oil money that disappeared in the final years of the nation's civil war. The size of Angola's oil revenues, however, had put the nation in a position in which it did not much care about the IMF's concerns; the Angolans could play the Chinese off the Americans and ignore the IMF and the World Bank altogether. In 2004, when the IMF held up a loan to Angola because of suspected corruption, the Chinese quickly offered Angola a replacement $2 billion loan; in so doing, the Chinese gained a major stake in Angola's future oil production. China essentially made an end run around the World Bank and International Monetary Fund policies regarding minimal standards of transparency, assessments of overall debt and fiscal policy, open bidding for contracts, and environmental-impact studies.

By 2005, Angola had become that largest supplier of oil to China, accounting for nearly 40 percent of that nation's African imports. Chinese companies arrived in Angola to build hospital, bridges, offices, railroads, schools, and roads, as well as lay a fiber-optic network and

---

[3] "Nowadays, Angola is Oil's Topic A," *New York Times*, March 20, 2007.

train Angolan telecommunication workers. In the capital of Luanda, hotel rooms were going for more than $200 a night; oil companies accounted for those hotels being completely booked two months in advance, and some company employees flew nonstop to Houston three times a week. With 18 percent growth year after year, Angola's economy was now one of the fastest growing, not only in Africa, but also in the world. Angola had become the second-largest oil producer in sub-Saharan Africa after Nigeria. Angola's oil and gas industries had attracted more than $20 billion in direct foreign investment since 2003. Its oil represented more than 40 percent of GDP and almost 90 percent of government revenues.

Zimbabwe

Zimbabwe was another story. In July 2005, despite many accusations of human-rights abuses against President Robert Mugabe, the Chinese government, in exchange for "mineral and other trade concessions," promised Zimbabwe an economic aid package. The Chinese foreign ministry said that China "trusts Zimbabwe's government and people have the ability to deal properly with their own matters," signaling clearly that the ministry believed that Mugabe's torture camps would not stand in the way of Chinese investments in Zimbabwean oil production or purchases of Zimbabwean oil. Hu was quoted as saying to Mugabe, "You have made major contributions to the friendly relations between our two countries. . . . I stand ready to have an in-depth exchange of views with your excellency on our bilateral relations." Several years later, in the face of international indignation, the Chinese blinked, and it appeared that they might seek to distance themselves from Mugabe, but they might only have been seeking a public disengagement.

Aiding or Abetting?

Because most of the world's major oil fields were already taken, in its attempts to ensure oil supplies from as many sources as possible, "China has ended up with the world's thugs: Sudan, Iran, and Myanmar. China has been particularly active in Africa."[4] Indeed, in Sudan's Darfur region, Chinese oil money and Chinese-made weapons have backed the slaughter of hundreds of thousands of people.

Thanks to oil discoveries throughout the continent, African oil producers will continue to reap huge financial gains. If oil were only to remain above $50 a barrel through 2020, then western African oil producers could still earn $1 trillion, close to double all the postcolonial aid given to African nations since their independence in the 1950s and 1960s. In the summer of 2008, oil prices shot to three times that level. That kind of money can finance a lot of coups, insurrections, and ethnic slaughters, but usually little of it trickles down to alleviate local poverty.

There is no doubt that the Chinese invasion of Africa has given that continent a completely different look. Ever since 1990, no foreign oil producer has had as much impact on Africa as China has. The question for the world is, has China's impact on Africa been positive?

For the most part, the answer seems to be yes. Some critics accused the Chinese of underbidding local African firms and of not hiring African workers. Others did not appreciate the offhand way in which the Chinese paid bribes to Africans or that China provided aid money without imposing any governance conditions. Still others expressed some concern that China's presence in Africa would drive away other overseas patrons who might have helped the Africans just as much—if not more than—the Chinese had. Nevertheless, in 2005, the Chinese invasion of Africa had resulted in a 5.5 percent growth rate for oil-exporting African countries.[5] By 2009, due to the world financial crisis, growth in oil-exporting countries was expected to fall to 2.4 percent.

---

[4] Nicholas Kristof, *New York Times*, April 23, 2006, at http://nytimes.com/2006/04/23/opinion/23kristof.html. In other places such as Cambodia's offshore oil fields, France's Total, a consortium led by Chevron, and CNOOC (the Chinese national oil company) have been racing one another to secure the lion's share of the estimated 2 billion-plus barrels. China appears to be leading.

[5] BBC News, May 16, 2006, "African Growth Prospects Improve."

The Quest for a U.S. Military Base in the Gulf of Guinea

With vital interests in Africa, the United States, as far back as 2002, began thinking of ways to protect its oil interests in the Gulf of Guinea. The idea of a military base, however, has met with some resistance: as much as African nations might understand why the United States wanted to protect its oil interests, they distrusted any move that smacked of imperialism. In 2008, the idea was still under discussion.

EAGER TO HELP IN AFRICA

The Chinese received the warmest welcome in Africa from Angola, but other Western and Asian oil powers had luck in other nations: France with Gabon; and Japan, India, and Russia with Equatorial Guinea, Chad, and Cameroon. In the largely agricultural Ivory Coast, China was financing loans to build a new capital in Yamoussoukro. In Chad, China was planning to build the first oil refinery and construct new roads, provide irrigation, and establish a mobile phone network.

No one was happier with the rising level of Chinese oil demand than the Africans, who were benefiting both from the rise in oil prices and the improved relationships they were enjoying with their newfound Chinese friends, who were building African roads, bridges, and dams at lower cost and in less time than Africans ever expected. Also, it is not surprising that the Africans were pleased when China cancelled $10 billion in bilateral debt owed by African nations.

However the situation developed—whether nations engaged in the quest for oil might get entangled with the Chinese or one or more of the major international oil companies became engaged in clashes or violence with one another—the new oil order was very different from the serene days of the nineteenth century and most of the twentieth century, and the power was shifting once again.

CHAPTER 4

Power in the Desert: The Gulf and the Middle East

For thousands of years, the economy of the Arabian Penin-
sula had been shaped by the culture of its nomadic tribes, who
grazed their flocks on the rough forage at the desert's border,
where rain was infrequent. The tribesman needed always to be
able to measure his animals' need to graze against their need
for water and the number of days it would take for the journey
back to the wadi.[1]

In the years when there was no rain at all, and the animals died
from lack of food or water, the tribal peoples began to seek alterna-
tive sources of income. Some of them became farmers, or weavers;
and some, craftsmen of other types. Some became merchants and
traders and took camel caravans across the desert, carrying goods
they might sell to pilgrims, while others took control of the wadis,
and those were the most successful, the ones who controlled what
came out of the ground.

The nomadic tribes that today collectively make up Saudi Arabia were not united under the rule of the house of Saud until 1932. It was then the middle of the Great Depression, and the kingdom's only source of income had been the fees it charged the pilgrims making the pilgrimage to

---

[1] Stream, spring, or oasis.

Oil for Gold

It was King Abdul Aziz Ibn Saud who had negotiated Saudi Arabia's oil concession with Standard Oil Company of California (SOCAL). Unwilling to trust paper money, he had insisted on payment in gold. Although the United States had just gone off the gold standard, the federal government made an exception and approved the payment in the king's chosen currency. For some years afterward, small wooden kegs full of gold coins were shipped each year to Saudi Arabia for oil payments.

the holy cities of Mecca and Medina. Those numbers had been declining significantly because of the global depression. Then, in 1933, oil was discovered on Saudi soil.

SOCAL negotiated a sixty-year oil concession to drill for and to produce the Saudi oil. The company invited Texaco to join in the deal, and this would be the beginning of what would later become the Arabian American Oil Company (ARAMCO). For additional capital,

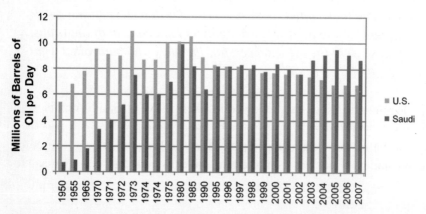

FIGURE 4-1 A Historical Comparison of U.S. and Saudi Oil Production

Source: United States Energy Information Administration (USEIA)

Exxon and Mobil were brought into the consortium. This is how the new oil order began: in the desert sands of the Arabian Peninsula and the boardrooms of the big U.S. oil companies.

It took until after midcentury for the Saudis to feel the economic impact of the discovery of oil, but eventually their lives were transformed. The kingdom's oil wealth permitted it to provide universal free health care and education to its citizens without collecting any taxes. Cities were built, and with them came schools, roads, and contact with foreigners, opening the eyes of the Saudis to the commerce and culture of the developed world.

There were those observers who said that, for a population that had only a short time ago been nomads in the desert, it may have been "too much, too soon." Some Saudis defensively turned more to Islam as a way to hold onto their familiar culture. The royal family, although also religiously observant, developed a fascination with Western ways. Some of its members were spotted at major auction houses buying art, at Harry Winston and Cartier's buying jewels, and in London and Monte Carlo buying hotels. All "unclaimed" real property belonged to the king, who was not only ruler of his country but also owner of most of it. That policy served the king well, because, in the once-nomadic country, vast parcels of land had never been "owned" by anyone. The result was that the royal family was able to appropriate 30 to 40 percent of the kingdom's oil profits as allowances for family members.

Distribution of oil earnings was a constant source of friction between the major international oil companies and the host governments. For the early years of the Saudi–American oil link, the Saudis seemed content to let the American oil companies run the show. Then, in 1950, King Abdul Aziz Ibn Saud, feeling that the Saudis were being discriminated against in the way oil profits were being distributed, began to pressure ARAMCO to divide the oil profits equally and threatened to nationalize his country's oil facilities. When the dust settled, the Saudis had abandoned their demand for nationalization, but they had been granted a 50 percent share of the oil profits.

Ultimately, however, there came a time when 50 percent of the profits was not enough for the Saudis. In 1968, Saudi Arabia's Minister of Oil Sheikh Ahmed Zaki Yamani gave a speech at the American University in Beirut in which he outlined expansive plans to increase Saudi control over its oil resources. He spoke of "participation" in the industry—as opposed to nationalization. No one was fooled by his language. His intentions seemed clear: he wanted to make the Saudi government dominant in Saudi oil production.

Within five years, the Saudis put "participation" aside and embarked on a program of nationalization, which, it hoped, would strengthen its hand. In 1973, the nation obtained a 25 percent share of ARAMCO, which it increased to 60 percent by the following year. By 1980, the Saudis finally acquired full control of ARAMCO and changed its name to the Saudi Arabian Oil Company (or Saudi Aramco). The company wanted to put to rest Saudi qualms that Americans behaved imperiously: showing respect for the local customs, the company handbook promoted the company as a proving ground for the ability of people of widely different cultures to work together.

The Saudis were bound to embrace such an approach. By beginning the process of nationalizing ARAMCO, the Saudis were setting a precedent.

OPEC

The Organization of the Petroleum Exporting Countries (OPEC) was created at a conference in Baghdad, Iraq, in September 1960 with five founding members: Iran, Iraq, Kuwait, Saudi Arabia, and Venezuela.

The founders were later joined by nine other nations: Qatar, 1961; Indonesia, 1962; Libya (Socialist Peoples Libyan Arab Jamahiriya), 1962; United Arab Emirates, 1967; Algeria, 1969; Nigeria, 1971; Ecuador, 1973; Gabon, 1975; and Angola, 2007. Ecuador suspended its membership from December 1992 to October 2007, and Gabon left OPEC in 1994. OPEC was originally headquartered in Geneva, Switzerland, before it moved to Vienna, Austria, in September 1965.

—www.opec.org

Prime Minister of Kuwait Sheikh Sabah Al-Ahmad Al-Sabah, right, and Saudi Arabian Minister of Petroleum and Mineral Resorces Ali I Naimi, as photographed during the OPEC meeting in Kuwait City, Kuwait, December 12, 2005. *Photo by Raed Nasser/Bloomberg News.*

Until then, no third world oil producer had questioned the authority of the Western major oil companies. None seriously considered seeking to reduce the financial power of the major powers because they alone possessed the advanced oil technology and knowledge needed for oil production.

The Saudis' triumph encouraged them to believe that oil power, if used carefully and selectively, could have a great impact on their country's political and economic life. A decade later, they were instrumental in going beyond their borders to form OPEC, an organization designed to enhance the power of the third world oil producers even more. At its formation, OPEC accounted for two-thirds of the world's 45 million barrels of oil per day.

By 1960, the Saudis' political clout was increasing in direct proportion to their oil production, but they nevertheless held out against domestic factions that were encouraging them to use their influence to build stronger relationships with their fellow Arabs and to punish Western oil consumers for siding with the Arabs' archenemy, Israel.[2]

By 1970, Saudi oil production had reached 3 million barrels of oil a day. Although the Seven Sisters had ruled the oil community from the 1930s, by the early 1970s the Saudis had become the world's largest producer of oil and had effectively taken over. The Saudis now had enough spare capacity to maintain oil reserves that allowed them to tighten and ease supplies to control prices. They needed to keep prices at a critical point: as high as the market would bear, but not so high as to push oil consumers into seeking alternative-energy sources. Tranquility reigned in the oil community, because those in power wanted it that way. America's oil dominance, however, was slipping away. In November 1970, the United States became a net oil importer. This was the first wake-up call for the nation. It was ignored.

On October 1, 1973, an article appeared in *Oil & Gas Journal* under the headline "U.S. Winter-Fuels Supply Situation Looks Precarious" that insisted a U.S. oil shortage was imminent. On October 6, 1973, a former secretary-general of OPEC issued a warning to the United States at the onset of the Yom Kippur War:[3]

> The Arabs now hold the keys to the energy and monetary crisis. They will know how to use both as a political weapon. Knowing this, the Arabs are in a position to solve their dispute with Israel on their own. How? Just put the squeeze on, not by embargoes or cutoffs. Just freeze output at current levels.

The boast became reality during the next few weeks. In a show of displeasure with the West over its aid to Israel during the war, the Arab oil producers began their oil embargo. One personality dominated the event: the controversial and telegenic Saudi oil minister Yamani.

---

[2] The hostility had manifested itself in terrorism in the early 1950s and then outright war in 1967 and 1973.

[3] *Oil & Gas Journal*, October 1973.

Yamani's long tenure as oil minister had given him considerable political power. He was a shrewd negotiator, businessman, and politician, whose own persona was his best public relations vehicle. He spoke English eloquently, sported a well-trimmed goatee, and wore his tailored English suit and Hermès tie as elegantly as he wore his flowing Arab *aba* and *keffiyeh*. He was a favorite on *Larry King Live* and did a good job of marketing the Arabs to the West. He also was the principal figure who had pushed for the Arab oil embargo and for the subsequent price hikes for the next several years.

And in the Rest of the Middle East . . .

By the 1970s, most Persian Gulf and Middle Eastern countries had emerged from Western control and bought or taken over major

A tanker entering a drydock berth at Dubai Drydocks World (DDW), in United Arab Emirates, on Jan. 9, 2008. DDW repairs ships and converts them into Floating Production Storage Offloading (FPSO) facilities for Gulf oil-producing countries. *Photo by Charles Crowell/Bloomberg News.*

ownership in the subsidiary companies that had been producing their oil. By the early 1990s, many of these subsidiaries had become completely nationalized.

In Iraq, British and Italians ran the show until 1961, when the revolutionary government of General Qassem nationalized 99.5 percent of Iraqi concession areas. The producing oil fields remained in Western control until 1971, when the Iraqi government nationalized the remaining interests, a move that resulted in major increases in revenues for Saddam Hussein's Baath party.

By 1911, Britain's Anglo-Persian Oil Company was producing oil in Iran, and SOCAL discovered oil in commercial quantities in Bahrain in 1932. Kuwait was the largest oil producer in the Gulf in 1953. Qatar came onstream with commercial quantities of oil in the mid-1950s, Abu Dhabi in 1962, and Dubai and Oman in the late 1960s.

The Future of Arab Oil

The United States had ignored one wake-up call when the United States shifted from being a net oil exporter to a net oil importer. Now it had a second one: the Arab oil embargo, which it also proceeded to ignore. American fuel consumption continued to escalate through the 1980s.

A senior executive at British Petroleum warned that, given the rate of increase in oil consumption, the United States would have to find four or five giant new oil fields—and soon. (Five more Prudhoe Bays a year would have done nicely.)[4] Sir Eric Drake, chairman of British Petroleum, issued a similar warning: too few new oil fields were being discovered, and oil production would fall in just eight years. By 1982, the Saudis were producing 9.8 million barrels of oil per day to the United States' 8.6 million.

The Saudis had come a long way from being nomads in the desert and a long way from recognizing only gold as the only "real money." They

---

[4] Prudhoe Bay, on Alaska's North Slope, was the gem of U.S. oil fields, producing more than 12.8 billion barrels of oil since 1977.

understood what the United States and the rest of the world apparently did not: that one day there would be an end to oil. Prudently, they had diversified their assets and moved significant amounts of their oil revenues into hotels, department stores, and office buildings in New York, London, Paris, and Hong Kong. They had shown foresight where the West had not.

CHAPTER 5

Testing the Oil System: The War, the Embargo, and Spare Capacity

On October 6, 1973, which happened to be Yom Kippur, the holiest day in the Jewish calendar, the entire country appeared to have shut down. As was customary for the observance, even many fairly secular Israelis were attending synagogue or at least staying at home and fasting.

At about two o'clock in the afternoon, Egypt and Syria attacked Israel. Some observers said the Egyptian and Syrian goal was to force Israel to make a unilateral surrender of captured lands; others, that they wanted to eliminate the "Zionist entity" altogether. Israel, in one of the young state's few unguarded moments, suffered severe losses in human life and equipment in the first two days of the war.

Following urgent appeals from Israeli leaders, the United States finally provided Israel with an airlift of military supplies, enabling the state to recover from its initial setback.

In response, Saudi Arabia led the Arab world in an oil embargo against the United States and other Western nations.

Sheikh Ahmed Zaki Yamani[1] was the key to the nascent oil revolution within the Arab nations; the Yom Kippur War provided the occasion for that revolution. In the opening hours of the war, the Arabs had an

---

[1] Later in 1975 the high-profile Sheikh Yamani would be kidnapped from an OPEC conference in Vienna by the high-profile terrorist Carlos the Jackal, who was demanding oil revenues to benefit the Palestinian resistance movement. After some high-profile negotiations, Yamani was released unharmed.

advantage. The Israelis, still euphoric and drawing the wrong conclusions from their lightning-quick six-day triumph over the Arabs in 1967, had become complacent. Warned that an Arab attack might be imminent, the Israelis had hesitated. They had considered a preemptive strike but decided that world opinion would be against them if they chose that course of action.

Syrian MiG-21s attacked Israeli jets, and the Saudis sent the strategically considered number of three thousand troops into the fray—too many not to be noticed but too few for the Saudis to be counted as an equal partner with the other Arab states in the war.

In the Sinai Peninsula, during the attack's first afternoon, Egypt caught Israel by surprise, knocking out many Israeli tanks that had been ill fit for battle.

Far to the north, Syria, relying on twelve hundred tanks of its own, attacked the Golan Heights. The Syrians were close to taking back the Heights, which had been lost to Israel in the 1967 war, and they were close enough to conquer some Israeli territory near the Sea of Galilee. The Syrians' new Soviet-made SAM-6 missiles blew Israeli planes out of the sky with ease.

As Israel absorbed the news of the attack, it seemed that the nation's very survival was in question.[2] Few in the rear could sense how precarious the situation was at the front. Israeli soldiers were reeling from the shock of the Arab assault. Five hundred Israeli soldiers had died that first day, a shocking figure for so small a population in so short a time. That precious little information came from the battlefront only added to the shock, gloom, and fear. One thing seemed clear to the Israelis: these were not the same Arabs who had fought with such little skill in previous wars.

The Israelis realized that they would have to rally their forces quickly if they were going to avoid disaster, and within a few days and with some and help, they turned the tide, regaining control of the Golan Heights, and recapturing that part of the Sinai near the Suez Canal that had temporarily fallen under Egyptian control.

---

[2] At the time, this writer was covering the war for United Press International as its Jerusalem correspondent.

A large part of Syria also was taken. Jerusalem remained untouched throughout the war.

But this was more than a local conflict. It was a war in which the Israelis were the proxy of the United States, and the Arab states were proxies of the Soviet Union. The two superpowers were pitted against each other on a small battlefield, raising fears of a possible worldwide conflagration.

For the past six years, the Soviets had been airlifting supplies to the Arabs, so U.S. President Richard Nixon and Secretary of State Henry Kissinger vowed to supply Israel with whatever it needed to avoid defeat. Thanks to those supplies, the Israelis were able to change the course of the war. When the Soviets saw how events were playing out, they countered by sending a naval force of seventy-one ships, including sixteen submarines, to the Mediterranean and putting their seven airborne divisions on full alert. The regional war was escalating dangerously as the Soviets felt that they and their Arab surrogates were losing the war. Some observers said World War III was inevitable.

On October 12, only six days after fighting began, the Israelis on the northern front were just eighteen miles from Damascus and threatening to invade the Syrian capital. Israel's twelve thousand soldiers and two hundred tanks under the command of General Ariel Sharon (a future prime minister), fighting along the southern front, swept across the Suez Canal (the existing Israeli–Egyptian frontier) along two different routes, surrounding the Egyptian Third Army and coming within twelve miles of Cairo. The two Israeli military actions—on the Golan Heights and at the Suez Canal—proved to be the turning points of the war.

The Arabs, looking for a way to strike back at Israel and the United States and tip the balance of victory yet again, were about to use a new weapon: oil. Saudi Arabia and the OPEC states were getting ready to declare an oil embargo against the West. Until then, the Americans had, often thanklessly, kept the price of oil manageable (though some Americans complained that prices had "skyrocketed" during the early 1970s from $2 to $3 a barrel). What effect would an all-out embargo have? Suddenly, oil consumers were made startlingly aware of their vulnerability.

On October 12, the chairmen of Exxon, Texaco, Mobil, and Chevron—the four American oil companies in ARAMCO—sent a memo to General Alexander Haig, Nixon's chief of staff, warning that any increased U.S. aid to Israel would adversely affect relations with Arab moderates. They cautioned that adverse relations with the so-called moderates might mean that oil prices would rise steeply.

On October 17, Saudi King Faisal made it official. He wrote to President Nixon, saying that the Arabs would impose an oil embargo if the United States did not discontinue its shipment of military supplies to Israel within two days.

Nixon's reaction was swift. Let the Arabs begin their embargo, he told his advisers; he was firm in his commitment to Israel. To show that support, he sent the U.S. Sixth Fleet of forty-nine ships, including two aircraft carriers, to the Mediterranean to maintain a state of combat readiness. With its own brand of decisiveness, OPEC raised the price of oil to slightly more than $5 a barrel.

Through most of the 1960s, ARAMCO's oil had been priced at $1.80 per barrel. On October 17, 1973, the Saudis announced a 10 percent reduction in their oil production and a total ban on oil shipments to the United States and the Netherlands. (Rotterdam was a main receiving port for Middle Eastern oil.) Before this, the Saudis had always chosen to release additional oil production onto the market with an eye toward keeping oil prices low to avoid harming the global economy. The Saudis knew that a 10 percent reduction in oil production would kick oil prices dramatically upward.

When the Arabs curtailed oil production by 5 million barrels per day, the other oil producers increased their output by 1 million barrels of oil a day. The net loss to the market was 4 million barrels, or 7 percent, through March 1974.[3]

With the United States unlikely to cave in to Arab demands to end aid to Israel, it seemed inevitable that the Arabs would continue oil-production cuts indefinitely. The next cut was by more than 20 percent, and by October 20 all oil shipments to countries offering aid and support to Israel had been embargoed.

---

[3] Seven percent may not seem large by 2009 standards, but it was a significant amount by 1973 standards, and oil prices quadrupled from $2 to $3 at the end of 1972 to $12 by the end of 1974.

For the United States, the oil embargo came at a particularly difficult time. Its spare oil capacity had only recently run out, and it had never before experienced a complete embargo. Americans were not used to being deprived of their cars or conveniences.

Those observers who followed oil events noted that the Arab oil embargo represented the first serious political muscle flexing by an oil-producing state. As oil nations had begun to nationalize their own oil facilities and as OPEC had grown more ambitious, politics had pressured the Saudis, and so the die was cast for tougher, unilateral, and overt coercive action.

The war had now been raging for nearly three weeks. With Egypt and Syria in deep trouble, the Soviets were urging the United Nations to arrange a ceasefire. Jim Akins, U.S. ambassador to Saudi Arabia, sent a message to ARAMCO, expressing his best guess that the oil embargo would not be lifted unless the political struggle between the Arabs and Israelis was settled in a way that satisfied the Arabs.

The war ended on October 22 with Israel as the clear victor. It had not only retained all the territory the Egyptians and Syrians had captured at the start of the war, but also, having gone deep into Egyptian and Syrian territories, had presented Egypt and Syria with the threat of a further Israeli incursion—into Cairo and Damascus—should they not agree to a quick cease-fire. Nevertheless, in the United Nations–arranged cease-fire, Egypt got its way: Israel would have to pledge to withdraw from all territories it had won during the 1967 war.

Egypt and Syria continued to fight small wars of attrition across their frontiers with Israel until Henry Kissinger arranged what were called "separation of forces agreements" between Egypt and Israel in January 1974 and between Syria and Israel the following June.

By the end of October 1973, the Saudis and OPEC were still waging their own "oil war." In December, OPEC announced a new oil price: $11.65 a barrel. There was panic at the pumps in the United States and Western Europe. Drivers were going from one gas station to another, seeking a few pennies' savings on the price of gas. In government attempts to enforce oil conservation, drivers were told not to use their cars at all one day a week. They waited for relief, but, much to their disappointment, the new, higher price was not a temporary aberration.

There was no solution in sight. Before the embargo, the United States had been importing 1.2 million barrels of oil a day; by February 1974, that figure had dropped sharply to eighteen thousand barrels. Americans were appalled and desperate. They blamed the Arabs, or the Israelis, or both for their predicament. Why should they have to sacrifice for people who lived thousands of miles away, who had brought the world to the brink of nuclear catastrophe, and who seemed unable to resolve their overall political conflict? It had always been conventional wisdom that, should oil prices suddenly rise, there would be some kind of economic meltdown—and in some parts of the American economy, there was.

Although the winter of 1974 saw oil shortages and inclement weather in the United States, Exxon's third-quarter profits were 80 percent higher than the previous year, and Gulf's were up 91 percent. Exxon's profit at the end of 1973 came to $2.4 billion. No company—or no industry for that matter—had ever had higher profits.

In March 1974, the embargo was finally lifted, but Americans' shock—at coming to grips with a new reality, of observing how much control a foreign government and multinational corporations could exert over the United States—continued for some time. The new reality was that the price of oil was unlikely to go down to pre-embargo levels. It was a humiliating time for many Americans, who could not believe that these people, whom they had written off as unenlightened and unsophisticated desert dwellers, now wielded such power over them.

OPEC seemed unable to enforce member quotas. During 1979 and 1980, when oil prices rose in response to the Iranian Revolution and the Iraq–Iran War, Saudi oil minister Sheikh Yamani had warned fellow OPEC members that charging higher oil prices would not *increase* their profits. Rather, it would have the opposite effect: it would reduce worldwide demand and thereby *reduce* their profits. The other OPEC members had refused to listen. From time to time, OPEC set lower production quotas, but rogue members defied the Saudis and produced more than their quotas, neutralizing the OPEC gambit.

In 1970, as it was becoming a net oil importer, the United States saw its oil production levels falling, slowly at first, by a half million

Why the U.S. Did Not Use Its Spare Capacity During the Oil Embargo

If U.S. spare oil capacity had been used during the Arab oil embargo, the oil-supply problem would have been ameliorated considerably, but by 1970 spare capacity had shrunk to 1 million barrels per day. Although the oil was flowing, the shrinkage had been below the radar of the oil watchers, but in 1970, although U.S. oil production hit a new peak of 9.3 million barrels a day, the maintenance of the spare capacity reserves had been neglected.

For the first time, the Railroad Commission of Texas[4] permitted 100 percent capacity oil production. The United States no longer had a choice. Consumption was rising, and production had to keep pace.

barrels between 1970 and 1971 and then to 9.6 million barrels in 1990 and 8.3 million in 2006.

Through the 1960s and the early part of the 1970s, the United States had a substantial amount of spare oil capacity that was supposed to be available to tighten or ease oil production to temper prices. From 1957 to 1963, the United States was producing about 4 million "spare" barrels of oil a day that could be released into the market if something went wrong—too much rain, a pipeline explosion, an unscheduled refinery outage. Even without its being tapped, just the knowledge that spare capacity was available had served to calm the markets. Indeed, America's spare oil capacity had contributed to the oil world's smooth functioning from 1960 to 1972.

The United States began to issue warnings that its spare oil capacity was declining, but in November 1968 the U.S. State Department surprised European governments at a session of the Organization for Economic Cooperation and Development in Paris by telling them that U.S. oil production had dropped to the point where it would no longer be

---

[4] The commission is the agency that regulates the Texas oil and gas industry.

able to maintain spare oil capacity at all; America's strategy of maintaining spare capacity was not being supported by production. The Arabs had proved that OPEC alone now had the ability to control oil prices—and no country had become as dependent on oil as the United States.

In March 1974, after the oil embargo had been lifted, the world began to seek alternative producers, if not alternative energy. Within a short time, more oil was coming from the North Sea than from many OPEC states. Oil prices stayed flat from 1974 to 1978, between $12 and $13 per barrel, lulling some people into complacency. There was now, however, a growing number of people who feared such a thing could happen again and who thought the oil-consuming countries needed to have a backup plan.

In December 1975, the Energy Policy and Conservation Act officially established the Strategic Petroleum Reserve (SPR) as a reserve

Crude oil being delivered to the U.S. Strategic Petroleum Reserve. The U.S. may make loans to refiners from the U.S. Strategic Petroleum Reserve to make up for supply disruptions caused by the weather, price inflation, or war or terrorist attack. *Photo by U.S. Department of Energy via Bloomberg News.*

of as many as 1 billion barrels. It was not much—certainly nowhere near the size of past reserves—but it was a start and some measure of protection against steeper oil prices. Later, during the 1980s and early 1990s when the markets declined, OPEC members decreased their own spare oil capacity.

As of early 1999, some 4.572 billion barrels of crude oil were being held in inventories, of which 572 million barrels were held by the United States, but the strategy seemed to be losing its effectiveness.

The Strategic Petroleum Reserve: Has It Become Obsolete?

In mid-November 2001, President George W. Bush set the goal for the Department of Energy to fill the SPR to its capacity—700 million barrels—to "maximize long-term protection against oil supply disruptions."

The SPR reached its goal on August 17, 2005, just two weeks before Hurricane Katrina. Two weeks later, Bush was able to authorize the SPR to lend oil to refineries whose operations had been affected by the hurricane. In addition, the president announced the sale of an additional 30 million barrels to maintain supplies and calm markets.

In May 2008, the United States announced that it was ceasing purchase of oil for the SPR, hoping that the announcement would have a moderating effect on oil prices, but prices continued to rise.

Has spare oil capacity become a thing of the past? Some analysts argued that the capacity cushion of the mid-1980s could not be repeated. The Saudis were trying to cling to a spare oil capacity of 2 million to 3 million barrels, but significant growth in demand would make that hard for them to maintain.

Increasing Demand and the Changing Market

Indeed, the increase in demand for oil changed the oil markets in the 1990s. From 1990 to 2004, global demand for oil rose by some 16 million barrels a day; but the increase in the non-OPEC supply amounted to only some 6 million barrels of oil a day, much of it coming from the Russians.

The difference between the increase in global demand and non-OPEC supply could only have been met by OPEC, which, while eager to help, lacked the spare capacity. Organization members did what they could with production, however, and OPEC supplied an additional 10 million barrels a day from 1990 through 2004. Nevertheless, the increasing demand brought about the gradual decline of spare oil capacity. Although in 1985 spare capacity hovered around 10 million barrels a day, in 2004 it dropped to fewer than 2 million barrels a day (2 percent of global oil demand).

The loss of spare capacity had strong implications for prices. Without the spare oil, the oil powers could not respond quickly and efficiently to a seemingly accelerating rate of shocks, whether political, climatic, or technical. One example was with the Iranian Revolution, when oil prices more than doubled, going from $14 in 1978 to $35 per barrel in 1981 during the Iraq–Iran War.[5] Another example was the period between 2003 and 2005, when the average price of oil nearly doubled, rising from $21 to $43 a barrel.

One reason for the shocks that Western oil producers felt in 1973 and 1979 arose from the paucity of available information about oil prices and about the oil industry in general. The profession of forecasting oil prices had not developed. Although the American Petroleum Institute published a weekly journal called the *Oil & Gas Journal* that included oil data, only oil industry insiders read it.

The Arab oil embargo signaled change. First, while it was happening, the embargo sent a message to the Western powers: although the Israeli–Arab fighting was isolated to the Middle East, Western powers that supported Israel could still be punished. Second, the embargo

---

[5] With the fall of the Shah of Iran in 1979, Iraqi leader Saddam Hussein smelled an opportunity either to take control of Iran's oil or to destroy it. When Iraq invaded Iran in September 1980, both countries together were producing only 1 million barrels of oil a day, 6.5 million barrels a day less than the year before. Iran never recovered from the terrible side effects of the revolution on its oil production, still only two-thirds of the level it had reached under the former Shah by 2008.

indicated to Western powers that control of the world's oil had passed from the Seven Sisters to the OPEC cartel.

If the Saudis were looking for proof of their assumption that oil supply shortages would lead to higher oil prices and economic disasters around the globe, they could take comfort in knowing that to some extent the assumption had proved true; the world had not suffered permanent economic setback; economies had not plummeted into chaos, but American oil consumers *were* dislocated by the embargo, and it did affect the U.S. economy.

For decades, oil analysts scoffed at the idea that any country or countries would use oil as a political weapon. The Saudis had proved

Strategic Reserves: Who Has Them and How Much Do They Have?

In 2008, approximately 4.1 billion barrels of oil were held in various strategic reserves, 1.4 billion barrels were controlled by governments, and the remainder was held by private industry.

Currently, the U.S. Strategic Petroleum Reserve is one of the world's largest strategic reserves, an estimated 700 million barrels as of April 2008.[6] Most of the remainder of the world's oil reserves are held by the other twenty-six members of the International Energy Agency: Australia, Austria, Belgium, Canada, the Czech Republic, Denmark, Finland, France, Germany, Greece, Hungary, Ireland, Italy, Japan, the Republic of Korea, Luxembourg, the Netherlands, New Zealand, Norway, Portugal, the Slovak Republic, Spain, Sweden, Switzerland, Turkey, the United Kingdom, and the United States.

Recently, other non-IEA countries have begun creating their own strategic petroleum reserves, with China having the largest of these new reserves.

—U.S. Energy Information Administration

---

[6] U.S. Department of Energy figures.

them wrong, but the Saudis were also wrong: they had always thought that if various national economies were to suffer setbacks because of higher-priced oil, they would also suffer disastrously. In the event, however, higher oil prices in the 2000s enriched the Saudis beyond their wildest dreams.

In retrospect, what was surprising was not that the Arabs had used oil as a political weapon, but that they had waited so long to use it. Like many other oil-producing states, the Saudis had been mesmerized by the clout of the Seven Sisters; had it not been for that, they might have deployed an embargo earlier.

The 1979 Iranian Revolution produced further hardship regarding oil. During June and November 1979, Iran produced only 2.5 million barrels of oil per day. At one stage, production nearly came to a halt. But if anyone needed evidence that oil and violence were becoming a lethal mix, Saddam Hussein's invasion of Kuwait in 1990 provided it. Here for the first time was one country acknowledging that it was going to war to shore up its oil supplies. When Saddam's army marched into Kuwait to capture that country's rich oil fields, few people doubted that he would stop there. Saudi Arabia seemed like an obvious next target; with its untested army, it also seemed like easy pickings.

The Saudis and other Gulf states were becoming all too aware that they should have some kind of formal U.S. alliance in the event that other states or even terrorists decided to go after their own considerable oil reserves.

"Today the national security interests of key oil producers, especially those in the Middle East, are much different from what they were a generation ago," said Ed Morse, former chief energy analyst for the now-defunct Lehman Brothers.[7] Linkages between the national security of the Gulf states and the security of supply in the West have always existed, but they were much less overt in the 1970s, when Arab countries distanced themselves from the United States because of its support of Israel.

"The Gulf War changed this in fundamental ways, especially for Kuwait, Saudi Arabia, and the smaller Gulf emirates," Morse

[7] Edward Morse, interview, May 29, 2007.

continued. "After 1990, the need to tie national defense and the survival of their states to a U.S. security guarantee was both clearer and more politically acceptable for these countries."

One indication that Kuwait wanted to have a stronger security relationship with the United States was its welcoming of foreign investment. Kuwait had no need for American capital, but if American companies were to invest in the country, then the U.S. government would feel obligated to protect the emirate. Or so the thinking went.

Equally eager to deepen its friendship with the United States, the Saudis sought to make sure that the United States thought it was a reliable and essential supplier of oil. Because the United States seemed now to be considering the Middle East "a bad neighborhood" and was seeking oil in the North Sea and western Africa, ARAMCO extended a hand and reduced prices to the U.S. Gulf Coast market. Caring less this time about maintaining high prices, the Saudis wanted to return to their formerly vaunted position as the top oil supplier to the United States. They had begun to realize their star was in decline.

CHAPTER 6

The History of Oil and the American Dream

By the late 1840s, sperm whales had been hunted to near extinction, and the cost of whale oil used for lamp fuel had climbed. Demand grew for new, inexpensive, safe illuminants and lubricants for the machinery of the Industrial Revolution.

At the same time, in another industry, salt mining, drillers in Ohio, New York, West Virginia, Kentucky, and Pennsylvania were plagued with a problem. An unwelcome by-product of their drilling—petroleum—was contaminating their wells, some of them so badly that they had to be abandoned. Samuel M. Kier, whose father had salt wells and who was therefore familiar with petroleum, began seeking a use for the product, and he began to distill petroleum into lamp fuel. "Carbon oil," as he called it, was so successful that he built a refinery with a five-gallon still in Pittsburgh.

By 1858, large quantities of carbon oil were being sold in New York City, quickly replacing other dangerous and more expensive lamp fuels. Petroleum from northwestern Pennsylvania became the chosen lubrication for the textile industry, and demand for oil drove the price from seventy-five cents to two dollars a gallon.

On Aug. 27, 1859, near Titusville, Pennsylvania, Edwin L. Drake struck oil in the first commercially successful well drilled specifically for oil. The technology used by Drake was not new; what was new was the concept that it could be pumped out of the ground like

*water. So was launched the modern petroleum industry in the
United States.*

                  —Pennsylvania Historical and Museum Commission

In its early days, oil was used mostly as a lubricant or, when distilled
into kerosene, as a lamp fuel. Homes were heated by wood fires, and
transportation fuel was firewood or wind.

Drake's oil well was only sixty-nine feet deep and produced only
twenty-five barrels of oil, but, 150 years later, the oil industry has grown
into the most important, and—in ways that were not appreciated for the
first 114 years—the most hotly competitive and controversial geopolitical issue of our time.

Historically, light had been provided by one fuel, and heat and
energy by another. Before the 1800s, light had been provided by torches,
candles made from tallow, and lamps that burned oils rendered from
animal fat. Whale oil, because it burned with less odor and smoke,
represented a significant advance, but it was very expensive. When a
clean-burning kerosene lamp appeared on the market in 1857, its effect
on the whaling industry was immediate.

The High Price of (Whale) Oil and Peak (Whale) Oil Theory

These days Americans complain about the high cost of oil as it has gone
as high as $145 per barrel in the summer of 2008 and hovered at $80 a
barrel in early 2010. Even at that price, it is still a lot cheaper than oil
was in the early 1800s. In those days before petroleum use, the whale
oil used in lamps cost as much as $1,500 per barrel (in today's dollars).
What was more worrying than the price was that some of the experts of
the period were forecasting an end to oil: soon there would be no more
whales.

Compare the price of whale oil with the price of kerosene. When
kerosene first became available in the 1860s, a barrel of crude oil

sold for about $90 a barrel in today's money.[1] By the 1870–80s, more efficient refining had brought the price down to about $20 per barrel (in today's dollars).

Fueling American Industry

From the Industrial Revolution through the late nineteenth century, coal was the chosen heating and energy fuel for the United States, Europe, and certain industrial sections of East Asia. It was cheap, available, and could be burned in the furnaces of factories, homes, trains, and ships. But oil consumption was gradually inching up on coal, and it was not happening accidentally.

John D. Rockefeller was a man who believed in the future of petroleum. He invested in the technology for more efficient extracting and refining processes, and he believed that anyone who could control the entire supply chain of oil would be able to dictate prices and make large profits. Rockefeller was right, but his vision was not passive. He was in a position to influence decisions that laid the foundation for the massive part oil would play in building the economy.

For oil to develop as an industry, it was vital to have a transportation infrastructure to transport oil. That was the railroad. The first locomotives were driven by wood-fired steam engines and then by coal-fired engines, but after 1900 oil began to be used for the first time as fuel. Now railroads were not only transporting oil but also burning it.

Railroads were an important component of the grand design for American industrialization, and so Rockefeller characteristically took an interest in the railroad industry as well. Railroads demanded steel for railroad cars as well as for track. In 1893, he helped develop the Mesabi iron ore range of Minnesota. By 1896, his Consolidated Iron Mines owned a great fleet of ore boats and virtually controlled shipping on

---

[1] Data from WTRG Economics.

the Great Lakes. He now had the power to control the steel industry. Sometimes, however, cooperation is more effective than competition, and, in 1896, Rockefeller made an alliance with the steel king, Andrew Carnegie. He agreed not to enter steelmaking, and Carnegie agreed not to touch transportation.

By the early 1900s, there was an alternative to rail travel as automobiles were mass produced. Soon the market was growing for economical automobiles and, with it, the need for additional infrastructure. Engineers found that a petroleum-based asphalt could create modern roads for the modern vehicles fueled by refined petroleum.

Americans now had the infrastructure—both rails and roads— to support railroads and automobiles that would allow transport unlike any seen before. The foundation had been laid for the business and economic expansion that marked America's remarkable growth in the twentieth century.

The "good old days." For many years, the oil world was ruled by the Seven Sisters (one of which was Exxon, formerly Esso) and OPEC. OPEC meeting in Vienna, Austria, on Wednesday, Sept. 10, 2008. *Photo by Vladimir Weiss/Bloomberg News.*

Of all the nations in the world, it was the United States that used oil to greatest advantage. Americans were neither the only ones to consume it nor the only ones to become so dependent on it, but they were the first and only nation to build an entire economy around oil. Developing nations came to realize that control of oil offered leverage, a competitive advantage, a political weapon.

John D. Rockefeller had created the Standard Oil Company in 1870, but by 1911 Standard Oil controlled so much of the oil industry that the U.S. government enacted antitrust legislation, forcing him to break up Standard Oil into thirty-four new private companies. From these companies, a group of sizable American and British oil companies emerged that collectively came to be known as the Seven Sisters. (See Chapter 1's sidebar on the Seven Sisters.)

During the decades after 1911, the Seven Sisters grew in importance. By entering into exclusive arrangements with local governments, they succeeded in preventing competition for the oil concessions. Of such importance was their expertise in oil that the oil-producing nations, in Anthony Sampson's neat phrase, "subcontracted part of their sovereignty" to the Sisters. Sampson compared the Sisters to nations when he wrote:

> Each of the seven had lasted more than fifty years, longer than many of their nation-clients. Their skyscraper headquarters, sticking up from their domestic surroundings, seemed to evoke a new world where nations themselves were obsolescent.[2]

Because the oil-producing countries had little inclination or ability to extract oil from their ground themselves, they were grateful to the Sisters for taking on the task; for their part, the Sisters were in a position to take advantage of weakness or innocence and carve out one-sided deals in their favor. With growing audacity, the Sisters dictated the terms.

---

[2] *The Seven Sisters: The Great Oil Companies and The World They Shaped*, Bantam, 1991.

The Sisters controlled the whole oil value chain—the oil fields, the storage tankers, the pipelines, and the gas stations—so neither the oil producers nor the oil consumers dared rock the boat. Because they maintained excess capacity, the Sisters had the ability to tighten or loosen oil supplies, thereby suspending the normal rules of supply and demand and controlling oil prices.

The Sisters became states within states, with tanker fleets larger than navies, and they were able to exert great influence on the foreign policy of all the Arab states as well as control half of the world's trade. The national governments had little to say; after all, they had signed concessions with the oil companies, and the companies set the industry standards for everything from how prices should be set to which oil fields should or should not be drilled and what each oil deal was worth.

Spurring the Sisters on was the U.S. government, which nourished an oil-driven economy second to none and was ideally suited to take advantage of the great benefits of oil.

The United States had sufficient natural resources—both mineral and agricultural—to avoid foreign entanglements. The U.S. government could make legislative decisions without fearing revolutions or coups. U.S. leaders did not suffer from the degrees of corruption and greed that infected the leaders of so many developing nations, and they could be trusted to allow the dissemination of oil revenues without siphoning off large amounts for personal use. But virtue and ambition alone would not have created the dynamic American economy without oil.

Flight to the Suburbs Creates More Oil Dependency

As the GIs returning from World War II married and began having families, there was a mass movement to the suburbs, and people wanted more and more of the amenities of middle-class living: washing machines, television sets, and air conditioners—and automobiles.

Rex Tillerson, chairman and chief executive officer of ExxonMobil Corp., speaks during a news conference in Dallas, Texas, on May 28, 2008. *Photo by Matt Nager/Bloomberg News.*

Families started out buying one car, but often found they needed a second. As a result, between 1948 and 1972, oil consumption tripled from 5.8 million to 16.4 million barrels a day.

The Americans were in a "golden period" of economic growth and development, but, without realizing it, they were on a dangerous course as the United States used more and more of its own oil. In 1970, the United States reached a milestone it should have heeded: it became a net importer of oil.

Suburbanization, the flight of people from the inner cities to the suburbs, sparked fresh demand for oil by making the car a virtual necessity. As the United States began mass producing the automobile in the early part of the twentieth century, increased driving was facilitated by the cheap price of oil. The number of motor vehicles in the United States rose from 45 million in 1949 to 119 million in 1972. Between 1945 and 1954, 9 million people moved to the suburbs. Between 1950 and 1976, the suburban population was 85 million. By 1976, more Americans lived in suburbs than in either central cities or rural areas.

In 1956, President Dwight D. Eisenhower signed the Interstate Highway Bill, which provided for a 41,000-mile superhighway system that crisscrossed the nation, and Americans took to the road. In the United States, a new word was coined—*motel*—to describe a hotel located near a gas station along one of the nation's highways. Oil made it all possible, and Americans went on an oil binge. The naive assumption seemed to be that the oil would always be cheap and readily available, the United States would always remain the largest oil producer in the world,[3] and the Seven Sisters would always be in control of international oil.

Nationalized Oil

Nationalization of the oil infrastructure in foreign oil-producing nations would have turned the tables on the Western oil companies at that time, but for a long time few of those nations had the audacity or the technical knowledge required for nationalization. Even though it took the lion's share of the profits, the United States also acted as a kind of international guardian, keeping oil prices secure and steady.[4]

---

[3] For a while, oil supplies seemed to be increasing. In 1955, industrialized nations produced 15.4 million barrels of oil a day, whereas U.S. domestic production was 6.85 million barrels a day; its 4 million barrels of spare production capacity was 26 percent of world output and 37 percent of U.S. production capacity.

[4] "What kept the oil world stable," observed Dr. Ronald B. Gold, international energy economist and consulting senior advisor to the PIRA Energy Group, "was American spare capacity."

It took until 1960 for the earliest and most powerful sign of an incipient nationalist awakening to come; that was the year OPEC was formed. The local oil companies watched developments carefully throughout the 1960s, and when nationalism came, in the late 1960s and early 1970s, it was still a surprise to some people.

The Venezuelans nationalized their oil industry in 1968, and Libya's Muammar Gaddafi began a process of nationalization of oil installations in 1970. Nevertheless, many thought that Venezuela's nationalization was an isolated event and that Gaddafi was a maverick and that these two events did not indicate a trend. Because those oil-producing states that had nationalized their oil facilities had done so as individual nations, their actions lacked the clout of a collective action.

Then, on February 24, 1971, Algeria nationalized 51 percent of its French oil concessions. On June 1, 1972, Iraq nationalized the Iraq Petroleum Company's concession, which was owned by British Petroleum, Royal Dutch Shell, Compagnie Française des Pétroles, Mobil, and Standard Oil of New Jersey. There were no retaliations, and these early nationalizations became the basis of national oil companies that went on to become world-class players such as ARAMCO of Saudi Arabia and Petrobras of Venezuela.

Until the 1980s, the key oil players had been in the Middle East and the Northern Hemisphere, but that was now changing. The center of gravity of world oil production began shifting to the Southern Hemisphere, to the developing world, to countries that were conflict-infested and corrupt at the highest political levels, a situation that would keep global oil production vulnerable to instability, volatility, and high prices. For the first time, the outlook changed from "calm, with occasional periods of tension," to "tense, with occasional periods of calm."

After World War II, the United States had entered into a kind of tacit agreement with Saudi Arabia regarding oil prices. It was increasingly clear that the United States would one day become a net importer of oil, and the Saudis committed themselves to the efficient, inexpensive, and uninterrupted supply: the United States "agreed" to purchase Saudi oil and to protect both the oil and the Saudis themselves. The tacit agreement held obvious advantages for both countries. No joint pronouncements were made; indeed, both parties were very cautious, even secretive, with each other. But the understanding existed nevertheless, and, though only implicit, it was strong enough to create complacency in the United States.

In 1974, the Arab oil embargo and subsequent oil price increase spooked Americans. They had thought they had an "understanding" with the Arabs. The American disillusionment, however, was brief: U.S. oil consumption declined to 16 million barrels per day by 1975, but it then resumed its climb, until 1979, when the Iranian Revolution caused another pullback until the early 1980s.

Complacency over Spare Oil Capacity

U.S. complacency over oil was never better illustrated than when the Shah of Iran visited the United States in 1969 to attend the funeral of President Dwight D. Eisenhower. When the funeral was over, the Shah paid a visit to President Richard M. Nixon, who had just taken office. At their meeting, the Shah proposed that Nixon consider creating a strategic petroleum reserve and offered to sell the United States a ten-year supply of Iranian crude—1 billion barrels—at the fixed price of one dollar per barrel.

Had any national leader shown up at the White House in the early part of the twenty-first century and made such an offer, no U.S. president would have hesitated more than a minute to accept it. In 1969, however, Richard Nixon huddled with his advisers for six months—and then finally decided that the idea had no merit. That the offer was rejected indicates how unimaginable it was to consider a future when oil would be expensive or difficult to obtain.

In 2005, U.S. oil imports reached 12.2 million barrels a day, and America's top oil suppliers were Canada, Mexico, Saudi Arabia, Venezuela, and Nigeria. Because some of these states were unstable, the United States was making some very risky bets. U.S. oil imports dropped to 9.6 million barrels a day in November 2009.

CHAPTER 7

Ethics and Oil

Beyond Petroleum . . .
. . . means being a global leader in producing the cleanest burning
fossil fuel, natural gas;
. . . means being the first company to introduce cleaner burning
fuels to many of the world's most polluted cities;
. . . means being the largest producer of solar energy in the
world.

—BP Ad, December 2000

*By some estimates, the BP ad campaign cost approximately $250
million. The message seemed to be that BP was, in fact, not an oil
company at all but an alternative-energy company.*

*Environmentalists saw red. "Greenpeace went ballistic," says Eric
Dezenhall,[1] who runs a public-relations firm based in Washington,
D.C., that has done work for major oil companies, In addition, says
Dezenhall, "Some oil executives thought that by spending all that
money to say essentially you're not an oil company, they would quiet
the media; but the campaign made reporters want to dig even deeper,
environmentalists too. I have tried to discourage petrochemical companies from doing ads that effectively deny who they are."*

*BP's rebranding of itself as the "Beyond Petroleum" company was
a bold act. Convincing the public that BP was not an oil company*

---

[1] Eric Dezenhall, interviews with author, September 2006 and November 2007.

*was a hard sell, especially, as Dezenhall suggests, "when 99 per-
cent of what you drill for is fossil fuel. People know that. That,
more than anything else, has convinced environmentalists that
oil companies are out there trying to brainwash the public."*

For the major Western oil companies, one obstacle to finding and
drilling for oil has been the issue of ethical double standards. Western oil companies, especially those in the United States, face enormous
public and legal pressure to be concerned not just about the environment but also about bribery and corruption, human rights abuses, and
corporate governance—whether in the United States, somewhere else in
the West, or in a third world country. Other companies, particularly
in Russia, China, or parts of Latin America, are not always bound by
such conventions.

In some cases, Western oil companies have gone into poorly developed areas and taken on the role of quasigovernmental agencies, providing health-care facilities, schools, and housing. Even with the best
of intentions, they have sometimes created controversies and resent-
ments that have divided local populations into those who benefit from
their services and those who do not. This is not to say that Western oil
companies have always behaved ethically, only that they are expected
to behave more ethically. For this reason, they perhaps sometimes
incur the higher costs of ethical behavior that they would not otherwise
have incurred were they not under the scrutiny of activist shareholders, corporate boards, or such groups as Amnesty International
(e.g., in Nigeria[2]).

The *Exxon Valdez* episode was about environmental damage,
public relations, and accountability. Exxon was expected to clean up and
restore what it had damaged and to compensate the victims. Arguments
might be made by the company or the victims about the fairness of the
dollar amount the company had to pay, but no one doubted Exxon's
culpability and responsibility and that it should pay a considerable

---

[2] *Oil For Nothing: Multinational Corporations, Environmental Destruction, Death and
Impunity in the Niger Delta.* Report from Essential Action and Global Exchange,
January 25, 2000.

amount in compensation. Humans' need for energy has always involved taking risks of varying types and degree. It seemed that the best approach is to try to minimize the risk as much as possible, and then, should catastrophe nevertheless occur, to respond quickly, ethically, and openly.

The *Exxon Valdez* Oil Spill

On March 23, 1989, the tanker *Exxon Valdez* departed the Trans-Alaska Pipeline terminal at 9:12 p.m. Pilot William Murphy maneuvered the 986-foot vessel through the Valdez Narrows with Captain Joe Hazelwood at his side and helmsman Harry Claar steering. After the vessel had passed through the Valdez Narrows, Hazelwood took over the wheelhouse. When the *Valdez* encountered icebergs in the shipping lanes, Hazelwood ordered Claar to take the tanker out of the shipping lanes temporarily to go around the ice. Then he turned over control of the wheelhouse to third mate Gregory Cousins. Then, for reasons that remain unclear, helmsman Robert Kagan replaced Claar, and Cousins and Kagan failed to make the turn back into the shipping lanes.

The *Valdez* ran aground on Bligh Reef at 12:04 a.m., on March 24, 1989. Captain Hazelwood was in his quarters at the time.

THE CLEANUP
The cleanup of the *Exxon Valdez* oil spill involved more equipment and more people over a longer period of time than any other spill in U.S. history. More than eleven thousand personnel, fourteen hundred vessels, and eighty-five aircraft participated in the first year of response beginning in April 1989 and continuing until September 1989. The response effort continued in 1990 and 1991, in the summer months, with limited shoreline monitoring in the winter months.

For months and years afterward, Exxon suffered a public-relations nightmare as the public watched television images of shorelines blackened with oil tar and shore birds struggling to swim or fly with oil-soaked feathers. People rightfully saw the event as a severe environmental

Oil spills are an ever-present risk, and responses to them differ according to the ethics of the nation or corporation responsible. The oil spill above shows firefighters and villagers cleaning up the crude oil leaked from the supertanker Hebei Spirit, in Taean, South Korea, on Dec. 8, 2007. *Photo by Seokyong Lee/Bloomberg News.*

insult to a pristine, ecologically important area that was home to many species of endangered wildlife. In the wake of the *Exxon Valdez* incident, Congress passed the 1990 Oil Pollution Prevention Act.[3]

WHAT CAUSED THE *VALDEZ* OIL SPILL?

After the investigation, the National Transportation Safety Board identified five factors that contributed to the grounding:

1. The third mate failed to maneuver the vessel properly, possibly as a result of fatigue and excessive workload.

---

[3] The act included such precautionary measures as requiring tankers to have double hulls.

2. The master failed to provide a proper navigation watch, possibly because of impairment from alcohol.
3. The Exxon Shipping Company failed to supervise the master and provide a rested and sufficient crew for the *Exxon Valdez*.
4. The U.S. Coast Guard failed to provide an effective vessel traffic system.
5. Effective pilot and escort services were lacking.

There was originally a judgment of $5 billion in punitive damages against the company, but ExxonMobil appealed the judgment, dragging the litigation on for years. Finally, on June 25, 2008, almost twenty years after the spill, the U.S. Supreme Court reduced the award to about $500 million. Exxon announced on June 30, 2009 that it would no longer challenge the courts.

Kazakhgate

Another far less tragic incident illustrates big oil's problems with bribery and governance ethics: this case has come to be known as Kazakhgate.

James Giffen was an American businessman and adviser to Nursultan Nazarbayev, the president of Kazakhstan, who, in his fifteen years of rule, had gained control of his country's oil wealth, pocketing a personal fortune at the expense of his poverty-stricken citizens.

Back in the 1990s, it was alleged, Giffen had paid $78 million in bribes to Nazarbayev and to Kazakhstan's former minister for oil and gas, Nurlan Balgimbayev, to win contracts for some of the largest Western oil companies to drill in the Kashagan oil fields.

In 2003, the authorities arrested Giffen at JFK International Airport in New York as he was attempting to board a plane headed for Paris. He was charged with bribing senior Kazakh officials to secure a favorable outcome to negotiations over the Tenghiz oil field, an action that violated the Foreign Corrupt Practices Act. The U.S. attorney presented evidence of international financial transfers, money laundering, and an array of domestic and foreign shell corporations, showing that

American oil companies, in order to gain access to Kazakhstan's huge oil reserves, had doled out money, expensive jewelry, speedboats, snowmobiles, and fur coats for the personal use of the Kazakh leadership.[4] The companies—including the Mobil Corporation (now part of Exxon-Mobil), Amoco (now part of BP), and Phillips Petroleum (now part of ConocoPhillips)—have denied any wrongdoing and say all their payments were made directly to the Kazakh government.

In October 2006, President Bush was preparing to receive Nazarbayev at a state dinner in Washington when the controversy blew up again; it was both an embarrassment and a dilemma for the U.S. government. The dinner was a diplomatic overture by which the administration was trying to strike a delicate balance with a country that had a growing strategic importance but also a record of corruption, flawed elections, and rights violations—including the killings of two opposition leaders. The government faced a dilemma. Critics said that holding a state dinner for a man who was said to be nothing more than a gangster illustrated the administration's willingness to sacrifice democracy when it conflicted with other foreign-policy goals.

Yevgeny A. Zhovtis of the Kazakhstan International Bureau for Human Rights and Rule of Law (an organization that has received financing from the American embassy and the National Endowment for Democracy) said, "There are four enemies of human rights: oil, gas, the war on terror, and geopolitical considerations. . . . We have all four."

While White House staff members were deliberating over whether the dinner would be held and which china would be used, a legal drama was playing itself out in Manhattan. Nazarbayev was named by the U.S. prosecutors in New York as an unindicted co-conspirator of Giffen's. The Bush administration finally capitulated in the face of mounting criticism and decided to cancel the state dinner.

On November 5, 2006, the *New York Times* wrote, "[T]he case against Mr. Giffen has opened a window onto the high-stakes, transcontinental maneuvering that occurs when Big Oil and political access overlap—a

---

[4] Christopher Pala, "Oil Scandal Hits Kazakhstan," *Washington Times,* May 17, 2003.

juncture marked by intense and expensive lobbying, overseas deal-making and the intersection of money, business, and geopolitics." As of the winter of 2009, the case had not been adjudicated.

Genocide in Darfur

For stories of human rights abuses, Darfur, in Sudan, remains the preeminent example. Sudan is believed to hold Africa's greatest unexploited oil resources, even greater than those of the Gulf of Guinea. In recent years, U.S. oil companies have mostly been barred outright from operating in Sudan, and other Western companies have been pressured not to operate there. (The Canadian oil company Talisman Energy, for example, is facing charges of "complicity in genocide and war crimes" in a U.S. court as of result of its past engagements in Sudan.)

Nations with greater energy demands than the United States or with fewer scruples—or both—have rushed in to Darfur to fill the vacuum created by the departure of the Western companies.

Four oil companies now dominate the oil industry in Sudan: China National Petroleum Corporation (CNPC/PetroChina), China Chemical and Petroleum Corporation (Sinopec), Petroliam Nasional Berhad (Petronas, a Malaysian company), and Oil and Natural Gas Corporation of India-Videsh (ONGC/OVL).

The Sudanese government's use of oil revenues to support its military campaign in Darfur has resulted in more than two hundred thousand deaths, countless women being raped, and other civilians being tortured or kidnapped. More than 2.6 million people have been rendered homeless by the conflict. Two-thirds of Darfur's population relies on humanitarian aid to survive. In the current civil war, the ongoing "ethnic cleansing" and genocide are being financed by oil.

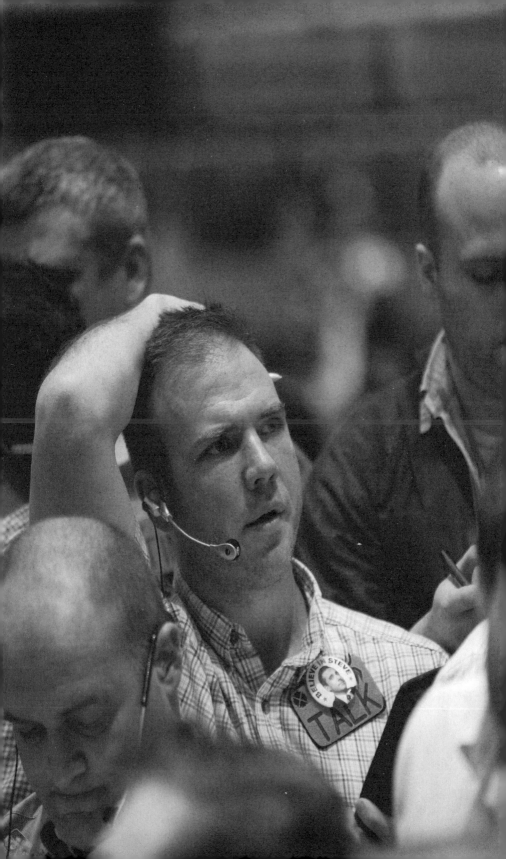

CHAPTER 8

Hedging: Insurance or Speculation?

The Arab oil embargo had been a wake-up call, if not to oil consumers in the West, then at least to producers, who realized now that a nation could turn off its oil spigots without warning and bring the economies of the United States and other nations to a halt. One way for the United States to address the problem was to create the Strategic Petroleum Reserve to hedge against unexpected political events. But other unexpected events were also a threat to oil-dependent economies: hurricanes, floods, dry wells, strikes, and civil wars. The oil companies needed another kind of hedge, a kind of insurance against any untoward event that could affect oil prices.

A trading platform that can act as a hedge for any commodity requires (1) *speculation* on the price of the commodity on a given date in the future and (2) *counterparties*—that is, two different parties to take the two different sides of the "bet." For such an exchange to provide sufficient liquidity to be robust, there must be a sufficient volume of trades, and the price of the commodity must be volatile.

During the time the Seven Sisters and OPEC had been running the show, oil prices had been mostly stable, and so there was little incentive to traders to take either side of a bet on prices. But times were changing.

Even without the 1974 oil embargo, there had been rumors in the early 1970s that the oil companies were deliberately causing oil shortages in order to drive up prices. Congress had responded by extending price controls on oil. Because Congress had jurisdiction only over *domestic* oil, however, the legislation of course affected only *American* producers, and imports shot up to nearly 50 percent of total consumption.

The embargo should have been America's wake-up call regarding its addiction to foreign oil, but it was not; sales of large cars continued to set all-time records.[1] By 1978, market volatility had reached critical mass, and someone with a little imagination could now make a case for an oil-futures contract.

Oil Futures

Emmett Whitlock, a sugar broker with E. F. Hutton, tested the waters in the commodity-futures exchanges to see whether anyone might be receptive to the idea of trading in oil futures. Few were—until he went to the New York Mercantile Exchange. By 1978, the price of oil was high enough, and the memory of the oil embargo fresh enough, that extreme oil-price volatility was no longer unimaginable. The exchange was willing to try the idea.

On August 24, 1978, Clarence Rosenbaum wrote in the *Journal of Commerce:*

> No. 1 heating oil and No. 6 industrial fuel oil . . . will be transacted on the New York Mercantile Exchange. . . . Backers of the new contracts . . . state that prospects for the new oil futures have evoked the interest of many of the leading independent dealers in the Eastern part of the country. These dealers, it is believed, will form the basis for heading operations.

On the morning of November 14, 1978, Michael Marks, chairman of the New York Mercantile Exchange (Nymex), and Robert Greenes, an important heating-oil dealer and president of the Empire State Petroleum Association, stood at the podium, waiting to introduce what would be the world's first successful energy-futures

---

[1] In both 1977 and 1978.

contract—for heating oil[2]—at the exchange's opening. Greenes was key to the creation of the heating-oil contract. Not only was he the head of a trade group called the National Oil Jobbers Council, but he was also an important booster of the contract from the commercial side of the business.

A small number of traders were there as well, and a few brokers were near the phones upstairs in their brokerage offices. At 10:30 a.m., a buzzer sounded, marking the opening of trading in the heating-oil market. It was a slow start. At the end of that first day, only twenty-two contracts had been traded.

Although oil speculation had barely limped out of the starting gate, the day nevertheless held great significance. In the beginning, these contracts attracted mainly wholesalers and large consumers

Traders in the crude oil options pit on the floor of the New York Mercantile Exchange (Nymex) in New York, on Sept. 22, 2008. *Photo by Jin Lee/Bloomberg News.*

---

[2] After gasoline, heating oil accounts for almost 25 percent of the yield of a barrel of crude.

of heating oil in the New York Harbor area, but its use soon spread to areas outside New York and to fuel sectors outside heating oil—diesel and jet fuel. With an exchange for futures contracts that could be traded, someone could, for example, purchase a futures contract for oil in May that would be delivered in July. Some market experts thought that a futures contract could have a moderating effect on the wild price fluctuations that sometimes had an adverse impact on an oil-dependent business.

WHO USES HEATING OIL FUTURES CONTRACTS?
Today, the futures contract is used by oil refiners, wholesale marketers, heating-oil retailers, and other major fuel-oil consumers—airlines, trucking companies, shipping companies—all of whom use it as a risk-management vehicle and pricing mechanism.

Fuel-oil distributors might use heating-oil futures or options contracts to protect portions of their winter-delivery commitments. If they can use the contracts to "lock in" prices for themselves, they can then turn around and offer their customers locked-in prices for their entire winter's fuel consumption.

Wholesalers might use contracts to protect their physical inventories or future oil purchases.

A commercial user of transportation fuel might use a contract to hedge against increases in the cost of diesel fuel, jet fuel, and No. 2 fuel oil.

Outside the oil industry, a trucking company, airline, or shipping company might use the contract as a risk-management tool for pricing, budgeting, and hedging fuel.

There are also nonindustry traders who use the contracts in a purely speculative way.

THE EXPANDING ENERGY BUSINESS
The new futures contract for heating oil was soon followed by other oil-futures contracts. Five years later, on March 30, 1983, crude-oil futures were launched.

In crude oil's first year of trading futures contracts, the average daily volume was 1,700 contracts, with each contract traded representing

1,000 barrels of oil.[3] Only seven years later, the daily average was almost sixty times as much—100,000 contracts, or 100 million barrels a day.

Now there were also futures contracts for gasoline, heating oil, and natural gas. The way the world conducted its energy business had been profoundly changed, and the timing of the new market for futures contracts could not have been better. OPEC had nationalized its oil companies and taken over pricing control from the Western majors. It hoped eventually to be able to manage the pricing of the entire value chain from drilling to refining and retail sales, but—given the mounting pressures on prices—OPEC members came to realize that they might be taking on more than they could handle.

In 1979, as a result of the Iranian Revolution, billions of barrels of oil were lost, and huge oil shortages arose. The price of oil rose sharply to $39 a barrel. The oil players were desperate for a way to have greater flexibility in pricing, and the futures market offered a solution: a way they could make price fluctuations less disruptive.

In 1979, when Iraq invaded Iran, even the resulting 3 percent cut in world supplies tightened supply enough to create another round of gas lines and a second "oil shortage." The price finally dropped in 1980, when Ronald Reagan swept aside oil price controls immediately after his election as president. Again, the futures contracts seemed to be accomplishing their purpose.

In 1982, the United States was in recession; as a result, by 1983, oil prices had dropped below $30 a barrel, and there were new oil producers. The Saudis' oil revenues were dropping sharply, and their market share was declining. They would have liked to increase their production to derive a consistent level of income, but instead they were trying to use their production capacity to moderate the market; they were deliberately and unhappily depriving themselves of oil earnings that others were getting. OPEC quotas had been set every few months, but the system was breaking down because some OPEC members were cheating.

Finally, the Saudis felt they had no choice; they had to turn on their taps. The increased production entered the oil markets in December 1985. Production soon increased from 2 million to 5 million barrels of

---

[3] Each barrel is 42 gallons.

oil a day. Almost immediately, the great oil collapse of 1986 began. By August, oil prices had dropped below $9 a barrel. It was now obvious to the world that the Saudis had lost their ability to regulate prices.

THE YEAR OPEC LOST CONTROL OF OIL PRICES
The oil crash of 1986 was a real jumping-off point, because it showed the world that from a price standpoint in terms of oil, OPEC didn't have a stranglehold. They couldn't just prop the price up when there was over-supply. And so the world had to look to the futures markets to hedge their risk, to lock in value.

> You weren't guaranteed that you could find an oil well and get rich like you saw in [the television program] *Beverly Hillbillies*. At $10 a barrel, you began to wonder whether it was profitable to drill for oil. Price became a huge issue. There were daily fluctuations in prices. Anyone could look at their screen and figure out what the price of oil was. That's why I think that 1985 is a crucial date, because that was when the (OPEC) cartel really started to lose control of oil prices.
> —oil trader and Senior Vice President Michael Hiley, Fimat Energy

SADDAM HUSSEIN'S WARS
Meanwhile, elsewhere in the Middle East, the traditional Arab–Persian conflict was being played out once again. Saddam Hussein of Iraq had attacked Ayatollah Khomeini of Iran in 1980, during what Hussein hoped would be a vulnerable time: the Iranian Revolution. Iran proved to be less vulnerable than Hussein hoped, however, and the war went on for eight years. Iraq was generally considered the victor.

By 1990, Hussein was reeling from the double blow of low oil prices and $75 billion in war debt. He had little chance of gaining forgiveness of that debt from other Arab countries. When Kuwait turned him down outright in his demand that it cancel the $75 billion debt, Saddam invaded that country, hoping to gain control of the Kuwaiti oil wells and perhaps extend his military action to the crown jewel of oil producers, Saudi Arabia. It was the summer of 1990.

With the invasion of Kuwait, oil prices rose sharply to $41 a barrel. With war's end, however, prices began to drop once more, and, by 1994,

One View: "Speculators Are in Control of the Market"

No government is paying any attention to what is going on. Speculators are in control of the market. It's not the oil company. It's not the Exxons of the world or the BPs or the Shells. It is speculators and financial players who are in control; they do not buy or sell crude oil for any use but they play the commodity. There's plenty of money to be made.

—Fadel Gheit, oil analyst at Oppenheimer & Company[4]

oil was $13 a barrel. A lack of volatility was no longer a problem for the oil-futures contracts.

THE FUTURES MARKET IN THE TWENTY-FIRST CENTURY

Today, with the different oil-futures contracts established, trading is open and completely transparent. The crude-oil futures contracts have not only become the principal benchmarks for calculating prices on the world market but also have provided a platform for players not even related to the energy markets. At times, the unpredictable speed and volatility of price movements have encouraged speculators to move into the market, pushing the spot and futures markets to dizzying heights. It was not only supply and demand that was an important price determinant but also supply-and-demand speculation. Serious questions have been asked about whether large traders and speculators could actually manipulate the futures market for their own benefit.

Although Nymex officials rejected the idea, the debate continued over whether open-outcry trading on the exchange, as opposed to electronic trading, directly affected oil prices. One analyst called the speculative market a "global gambling hall."

Some critics said the futures markets were being manipulated, but that outright manipulation seemed unlikely, although there

---

[4] Fadel Gheit, interview with author, September 5, 2006 and May 18, 2007.

"We Shot All the Slow Rabbits"

In the United States, as the saying goes, "we shot all the slow rabbits." Finding oil did not guarantee riches. There are still some slow rabbits elsewhere in the world, Russia being one place. A slow rabbit is like a shallow oil well that you can find without a lot of expense. Right now, if you want to develop oil in American waters, in the Gulf of Mexico, you are drilling two miles down under water. That's billions of dollars to develop a platform in two years—then it gets knocked over by a hurricane.[5]

—Oil analyst Michael Hiley[6]

undoubtedly was speculation. There were far too many participants with widely divergent interests who traded on a daily basis. It would have been nearly impossible for them to get together and conspire to move the market. No one "market maker" existed; rather, hundreds participated every day.

Exchange officials insisted that market movements were simply the volatile behavior of a free market. The sheer quantity of trades and the relatively primitive trading technology in the market's early days reinforced that view. The reporting systems were in place, and the president of Nymex himself signed off on all transactions. Any person holding more than fifty contracts in a day was to be reported both to the exchange president and the Commodity Futures Trading Commission. The requirements for trading were clearly defined. The amount of cash that had to be posted to obtain a position in the spot market within one month from the trade date was 50 percent of the value of the

---

[5] On August 29, 2005, Hurricane Katrina swept through the Gulf of Mexico. The storm, with 1,836 casualties, was not only one of the deadliest, but also one of the costliest in U.S. history. It took as long as a year to get some oil platforms back online.

[6] Michael Hiley, interview with author, May 17, 2007.

contract, roughly $6,000. The margin usually fell between 5 percent and 10 percent but was determined by the exchange president. Edward L. Morse, former managing director and chief energy economist for Lehman Brothers, says that the speculation that exists today has been made possible by "the incredible growth of liquidity that [now] exists in these futures contracts."[7]

Speculators might affect volatility, and they might even push prices up or down at any given time, but at the end of the day, they are *reac*tive, not *pro*active. In the twenty-first century, as it becomes more difficult to find oil and more difficult still to avoid supply disruptions, it is imperative for oil players to have the ability to keep prices manageable. The oil-futures market makes that possible.

---

[7] Edward L. Morse, interview with author, May 29, 2007.

CHAPTER 9

How Much Oil Is Left . . . and How Willing Is the United States to Drill for It?

In 1956, Dr. M. King Hubbert, a geophysicist employed by Shell Oil, postulated that fossil fuel production (oil, coal, and natural gas) in a given region over time would follow a bell-shaped curve. After fossil fuel reserves were discovered, extraction would start and more efficient facilities would be installed. Production would increase exponentially at first, but eventually a peak output would be reached and production would slow until it approximated an exponential decline. Peak output would occur in approximately 1970. With improved technologies and additional deposit finds, the right shoulder of the curve could be stretched, but the basic premise would not change: it would take us decades, rather than centuries, to exhaust the bulk of the energy that had been stored within the Earth in the preceding 500 million years. If we use Hubbert's curve and projected dates, the end of the petroleum age would occur in approximately 2060 to 2070.

American oil experts had largely agreed that, as of 1950, between 50 billion and 60 billion barrels of oil had been found and burned in the continental United States. They also largely agreed that, as of 1950, 150 billion to 200 billion barrels of oil still existed in the ground.[1]

---

[1] That estimate was increased to 590 billion barrels in the early 1960s.

The conventional wisdom was that enough oil existed for several more generations, and yet this man was defying conventional wisdom.

If what Hubbert said were true, then 90 percent of the recoverable oil in the lower forty-eight states would disappear by 1999. It was a startlingly unorthodox conclusion from someone who was supposed to be a respected geophysicist.

Even today, the oil industry is divided over Hubbert's theory. Saudi Arabia claims it could pump oil at the current rate for more than a century. Exxon's chief executive officer, Rex Tillerson, claims there are "abundant oil resources" and that the world might have 3 trillion barrels of oil left, three times more than has been used to date and more than twice the remaining reserves postulated by Hubbert's model.

Of course, it is in the interest of oil producers for the world to think that abundant energy reserves remain. Otherwise, oil consumers might seek alternative forms of energy.

Hubbert's speech, outlining his "end of oil" theories, was printed in 1949, but the oil industry hardly took notice of it at the time. When he revived his ideas at the 1956 meeting of the American Petroleum Institute in San Antonio, his speech caused an uproar, and many in the oil industry were incredulous.

Other, earlier forecasters had studied the future of oil, and many, like the one who had argued that no more oil existed in the entire state of Texas, were ludicrously wrong. But Hubbert's views could not easily be swept aside. His reputation grew to legendary proportions, and President John F. Kennedy appointed him as an adviser on the future of natural resources. By the time the energy crisis erupted in

An End to Oil?

Of the ninety-eight oil-producing countries in the world, sixty-four are thought to have passed their geologically imposed production peak; of those, sixty are in terminal production decline.

the 1970s, Hubbert's celebrity was almost cultlike, but the implications of what he had calculated had not sent any major energy group scurrying after windmills or making ethanol.

The notion that the world was running out of oil had not started with Hubbert. There had been predictions of an imminent oil famine in the early days of oil in the United States, especially in the late nineteenth century, when oil production at those first Pennsylvania wells started to decline. Then oil was discovered in east Texas, and the yield from those oil fields had been so abundant that the Texas Railroad Commission was forced to cap production to support prices.

Hubbert's critics pointed to "the facts on the ground" as better evidence of the durability of oil than scientific theories. How else to explain that even though oil geologists in the mid-1940s had put the figure of total oil reserves at 100 billion barrels, a mere decade and a half later the figure had increased two and a half times?

There is no doubt that, at the time he first expressed his peak-oil theory, Hubbert got a lot of flak—but he was mostly vindicated in 1970, the year he had predicted as the peak year, when oil production in the United States indeed began to decline.

Proven Versus Probable Oil Reserves

How is it that the so-called facts on the ground, the figures for proven oil reserves, can increase over time? Historically, one reason has been a positive development: there have been significant new oil finds. Too often, however, the reason is one not much discussed: oil-reserve figures have a tendency to be somewhat amorphous because each company or nation provides its own proven oil-reserve figures, and each one has its own accounting methodology for *proven* as opposed to *probable* oil reserves. Oil accounting methods had never been regulated or brought into any sort of consistent framework.

Reserves calculations are categorized as either *proven* or *probable.*

Proven reserves are those oil reserves that, by analysis of geological and engineering data, can be estimated with reasonable certainty

Democratic Senator Dianne Feinstein of California questions a witness during a
Senate Energy and Natural Resources Committee hearing on oil leaks at BP Plc's oil
pipeline in Alaska, Sept. 12, 2006. *Photo by Carol T. Powers/Bloomberg News.*

to be commercially recoverable from known reservoirs and under
current economic conditions, operating methods, and government
regulations.

Probable reserves, on the other hand, are reserves that geological and engineering data suggest were more likely than not to be
recoverable.

The distinction between these two categories is subjective, not abso-
lute. In addition, some factors, even with a company's best intentions,
can change over time: a particular technology that might not be
cost-efficient at one per-barrel price of oil might *become* cost-efficient
if the price of oil rises sufficiently. A new, cheaper production technology might be invented that did not exist when the first calculation
of reserves was made.

Because disclosure of a firm's proven and probable oil reserves
is a key performance indicator in the oil and gas industry, such
figures have a significant influence on share price, a not insignificant

consideration when the firm is subjectively calculating its own reserves.[2]

The Environmental Movement and the Peaksters

There was another political trend that emerged about the early 1970s that would also have an impact on the oil picture: the environmental movement. One early indication of a newly awakened environmental consciousness was a book published in 1972, *The Limits to Growth: A Report for the Club of Rome's Project on the Predicament of Mankind*. Its central theme was that, if several trends in population, pollution, food production, energy consumption, and resource depletion (including oil and natural gas) panned out, then industrialized countries' growth would become unsustainable, and the population of the Earth would simply stop growing within one hundred years.

Eventually, as a result of the growing concern over the environment, the United States decreased its use of coal and began to rely on cleaner-burning oil. The search for oil intensified, including offshore exploration, until an oil spill occurred off the California coast and President Richard Nixon's administration ordered an end to California's offshore exploration and production. With the rise of concern for the environment, there were more and more areas that would never be drilled, decreasing the world's available reserves. That people were now starting to pay attention to the peaksters' message was a significant point in the evolution of public attitudes toward both oil and the environment.

In 1977, oil was finally produced at Prudhoe Bay, in Alaska, and both sides of the peak-oil debate closely watched the evolution of production. The field had been discovered in 1968 and came onstream

---

[2] In 2004, the Royal Dutch Shell group of companies acknowledged it had downgraded the amount of its proven oil reserves by a significant 20 percent to 25 percent. The restatement, prompted by an aggressive Securities and Exchange Commission probe, led to the resignation of Shell's chief executive, Philip Watts.

nine years later. Since then, it has yielded more than 11 billion barrels of oil. By 2006, oil writers were suggesting it was near depletion. Production in 1988 had been 722 million barrels per day. By 2006, it had fallen to 264 million barrels; and by late 2007, production was 650,000 barrels. Prudhoe Bay had followed the Hubbert curve, which had been telling the same story going back to the 1940s. Hubbert's followers were now being taken more seriously.

In 2005, the late author and social commentator Kurt Vonnegut, although certainly no oil expert, nevertheless captured the growing body of public opinion when he told the Associated Press, "I like to say that the fifty-first state is the state of denial. It's as though a huge comet were heading for us, and nobody wants to talk about it. We're just about to run out of petroleum and there's nothing to replace it."

Not everyone agreed. ExxonMobil placed newspaper ads that ridiculed the peak-oil theory. The peaksters, they said, were alarmists. All told, said the ad, the world probably had 4 trillion barrels of oil left, four times the amount that had been used thus far. ExxonMobil said its geologists believed that global oil production would keep rising through 2030. On the other hand, was it not self-serving for oil companies to try to convince the public that oil was so plentiful that there was no need to seek alternative energies? What about new technologies that would make it possible to recover oil that had not previously been recoverable?

Author and social critic James Kunstler thinks that

[what peak-oil theorists say] comports with reality. Not only does [believing] the peak [theory] mean we're going into a remorseless decline altogether, [but also that] the supplies during that decline will be of grades of oil that are less and less good. . . . Ever since 1970, we've had less and less control and fewer and fewer resources. This then is a story of America's losing control of the primary resource that drives civilization— oil. Unfortunately, we're in an almost hopeless situation. . . .[3]

---

[3] Jim Kunstler, interview with author, October 4, 2006.

Daniel Yergin, chairman of Cambridge Energy Research Associates (CERA), takes a third view. He believes that immediate oil production will neither increase nor decline, but will instead reach an "undulating plateau" sometime after 2030, for one or more decades, before declining slowly. The global production profile, says Yergin, will not be a simple logistic or bell curve, as postulated by Hubbert, but be asymmetrical. The slope of decline will be more gradual than the rapid rate of increase and be strongly skewed past the geometric peak.

During the period of the plateau in later decades, according to the CERA analysis, demand growth would likely no longer be largely met by growth in available, commercially exploitable natural oil supplies. Nontraditional or unconventional liquid fuels such as the production from heavy oil sands, gas-related liquids (condensate and natural-gas liquids), and liquids made from coal will need to fill the gap.

It was difficult, said many analysts, to predict a peak when new information and better technology could push back the date. In 1997, British geologist C. J. Campbell partnered with Jean Laherrere, a retired French geophysicist who had worked for Total for twenty-five years, to analyze production profiles for countries around the world. According to Campbell, he and Laherrere concluded that global oil production was nearing its zenith. Popularizing their cause was their *Scientific American* article, "The End of Cheap Oil." "The world is not running out of oil, at least not yet," they wrote. "What our society does face, and soon, is the end of the abundant and cheap oil on which all industrial nations depend." Because the United States and global economies required energy to fuel their constant growth, perhaps the real question should not have been when we would *run out* of oil, but when would we decide to *stop increasing* oil production because of either environmental or cost considerations.

Finally, in 2005, the U.S. Department of Energy commissioned Dr. Robert Hirsch, a much-admired physicist, to write a report on whether the notion of peak oil was real and, if so, what could be done to mitigate the situation. Hirsch wrote that the notion was indeed real and that the peak of global oil production could occur within twenty years. In his introduction, he explained:

> The peaking of world oil production presents the U.S. and the world with an unprecedented risk management problem. As peaking is approached, liquid fuel prices and price volatility will increase dramatically, and, without timely mitigation, the economic, social, and political costs will be unprecedented. Viable mitigation options exist on both the supply and demand sides, but to have substantial impact, they must be initiated more than a decade in advance of peaking.

Whenever it occurred, Hirsch's report continued, the consequences would be huge, and the U.S. government should take control of the situation and begin a national energy program to help transition to alternative fuels.

Occasionally, large American institutions give the impression that they are eager to push alternative sources of fuel. When spokespeople come from the oil industry itself, public confusion ensues: it seemed counterintuitive for oil companies to support peak-oil theories. In 2005, Chevron actually ran a series of full-page ads in U.S. newspapers that focused on surging oil consumption, asserting that

> [i]t took us 125 years to use the first trillion barrels of oil. We'll use the next trillion in 30. . . . One thing is clear: the era of easy oil is over. . . . We can commit to working together, and start by asking the tough questions: How do we meet the energy needs of the developing world and those of industrialized nations? What role will alternative energy sources and alternative energies play? What is the best way to protect our environment? How do we accelerate our conservation efforts?

In 2006, Thierry Demarest, chief executive officer of Paris-based Total S.A., told the World Gas Conference in Amsterdam that global oil production would peak in 2020. Perhaps the oil companies were finding that denying the end-of-oil theory was flying in the face of growing public opinion.

Nevertheless, regardless of how each oil company's public relations group decided to position itself, there seemed to be relatively little that the major companies were actually doing to prepare for the end of oil. One thing that was certain was that every dollar invested in alternative-energy sources was a dollar taken away from oil exploration and production, and the majors were making huge profits from oil.

Members of Congress would have to be the source of a transformation to alternative-energy sources. Most, however, sat silently while the end-of-oil debate raged on. Rep. Roscoe Bartlett (R-Maryland) formed the Congressional Peak Oil Caucus to consider solutions to the end of oil, but he has not had many supporters. Perhaps rising prices will be the only catalyst for change.

Bartlett favors immediate action to promote and implement alternative-energy sources: "We've blown 30 years since 1980," he says. "We knew that Hubbert was right about the U.S. . . . We need a total commitment as we did with World War II and putting a man on the moon."

Some oil analysts point out that it is the high price of oil that has given the peaksters the platform to speak from. If oil were still at $20 per barrel, no one would have talked about peak oil, they argue. Renewable-energy enthusiasts existed in the early 2000s, but they were plagued by the usual bugaboo of start-up businesses: prices were too high to garner efficiency of scale.

Many alternative-energy sources have flaws:

- the use of ethanol inflates food prices;
- nuclear energy looks promising, but those who remember Chernobyl and Three Mile Island find it difficult to be enthusiastic about going nuclear;
- solar energy involves the construction and installation of solar panels, but no one knows if the power generated will be sufficient; and

Galileo and the Paradigm Shift

Dan Miner, peak-oil theory activist and senior vice president for business services of the Long Island City Business Development Corporation, has an urgent view with a historical parallel.

"The implications of fuel depletion are extremely disturbing," says Miner. "Galileo told medieval church leaders the earth revolved around the sun; it was a paradigm shift. They said, 'We're going to have to kill you. What you said was heretical.' The idea that our fossil fuels, on which we are so dependent, are soon to be permanently expensive is frightening, heretical; it's a dangerous concept. What I'm arguing is that we have to grapple with it, take it seriously, because, if we continue to ignore it, pretend it doesn't exist, and then just wait for the consequences to unfold, we won't have time to adapt, and it's all going to be an emergency."[4]

The end of oil is an ugly message that nobody wants to hear: it's bad for business, and it says that the conventional way of doing things and the era of easy prosperity are over.

- windpower, the solution favored by oil entrepreneur T. Boone Pickens, is unproven in ease of execution and cost efficiency.

Some strategists insist that it is simply a matter of putting more cash into alternative-energy research. For that, however, we must have a consensus not only about committing to alternative energy but also about deciding which alternatives we should pursue.

Ian Bremmer is a political scientist who specializes in U.S. foreign policy and global political risk. He is also the president of New York–based Eurasia Group, a global political risk consultancy.

---

[4] Dan Miner, interview with author, September 7, 2006.

"The United States," he notes, "does not have the ability, like China, to tell its people, 'You're going to have to deal with nuclear energy whether you like it or not.'" In fact, it is the United States' very democratic process that keeps it from reacting quickly to a massive challenge like the current one.

CHAPTER 10

Oil for the Lamps of China . . . and India

In the seventy-five years since the book was published, the title Oil for the Lamps of China[1] *has become a catch phrase for expansive American dreams of exploiting the vast China market. The story was a drama about corporate treachery, and the main character was an eager and idealistic young American businessman who had been sent by the American oil company he worked for to penetrate China's untapped market. He believed he could bring progress to China via oil and oil lamps, but ended up being caught between the dogmatic fervor of Chinese revolutionary nationalism and the heartlessness of the company on whom he had staked his career.*

The world has long been concerned with how oil might affect China, but China has responded in its own time and at its own pace. Its time is now, and its pace is having a global impact.

During most of the twentieth century and at the beginning of the twenty-first century, many Americans thought of the Chinese as dangerous and backward. They could, it was believed, be a threat to the West, given their hostility and nuclear capability, and their values had little to do with American values.

Interestingly, the Chinese had some of the same stereotypes about the West; they referred to foreigners as "barbarians" and eschewed cultural

---

[1] Alice Tisdale Hobart, 1934. *Oil for the Lamps of China.*

or mercantile relationships with them out of fear that their own ideology would become corrupted.

For many years, the Chinese embraced an isolationist policy, and the society was mostly agrarian. In 1959, however, they discovered oil in the Daqing oil fields under the Manchurian grasslands. Although they could use only some of it at the time, it seemed that the surplus could provide a good revenue stream.

China's course changed in 1978, however, when Deng Xiaoping assumed power. He reached out to the West to introduce industrialization, technology, and modern business methods to China to shore up the financial foundations of his communist state.

As an indication of the abruptness of China's transformation, consider that, as late as 1990, the bicycle was by far the most popular form of transportation in China. A scant twenty years later, in cities like Shanghai, air pollution from automobiles has become a problem and nothing seems capable of stopping—or even slowing—the rapid rise of a car culture. A car culture, as the United States has learned, is a beast that must be fed, and, consequently, China's newly built infrastructure and factories required more fossil fuel than China ever imagined, accounting for about 12 percent of the world's energy demand and four times the global rate of oil consumption.

It was 1984 when Deng Xiaoping extended his invitation to the West and said that China was open for business. On June 30 of that year, Deng Xiaoping addressed the Japanese delegation at the Council of Sino-Japanese Non-Governmental Persons, declaring:

> We welcome foreign investment and advanced techniques. Management is also a technique. Will they undermine our socialism? Not likely, because the socialist sector is the mainstay of our economy. Foreign investment will doubtless serve as a major supplement in the building of socialism in our country. And as things stand now, that supplement is indispensable.

Slowly but steadily, foreign investment came to China. Visitors in the early 1990s could see skyscrapers dotting the landscape in cities from Shanghai to Beijing or visit a new Wal-Mart. As for technology,

Comparative GDP Growth: China Versus the United States

Year	China (%)	U. S. (%)
2004	10.1	3.1
2005	9.9	4.4
2006	11.1	3.2
2007	11.4	3.2

Sources: U.S. data: U.S. Department of Commerce, Bureau of Economic Analysis.China data: National Bureau of Statistics, China Statistical Yearbook 2004, National Bureau of Statistics of China Plan Report, www.chinability.com.

Microsoft and Google were eager to break in to the Chinese market, and they have been willing to make compromises to accomplish their goals. Although much of its 1.3 billion-person population remains poor, China's emergent middle class is projected to reach 100 million by 2010—13 percent of the nation!

By 1993, the Manchurian oil fields were no longer sufficient to keep pace with the country's astounding growth, and China became a net importer of oil. Since then, its economic progress has been so rapid that the search for overseas oil sources has become increasingly frantic—even while the country's environmental experts warn of impending ecological and economic doom if the Chinese continue on their current course. The rest of the world has been equally concerned about the China effect: on global oil supplies, on ecology, on geopolitics, and on economics.

By 2004, oil producers and consumers, traders, and analysts were astounded to see Chinese oil demand rise to 1 million barrels a day. China now needed overseas investment to secure future oil supplies. Needing a six-hundred-mile pipeline from Kazakhstan to China, the Chinese committed themselves to building it—eastward—although the United States would have preferred that the pipeline run westward to Murmansk at the Barents Sea, which would presumably have been cheaper and more convenient for the United States.[2]

---

[2] "Can Pipe Dreams Turn into Reality?" *Los Angeles Times*, July 18, 2004.

The pipeline was completed in December 2005 and began pumping on May 25, 2006. By the end of 2006, it was bringing two hundred thousand barrels of oil a day to China. But that was not enough, according to oil analyst Larry Goldstein.

> [2004] was the year . . . we crossed a threshold, where you went from surpluses to tenuous balance. Production problems somewhere were made up by producing somewhere else. You could run more crude in someone else's facility and discretionary product inventories, which is your first line of defense. You had those safety valves—those cushions, those shock absorbers. In 2004, those shock absorbers disappeared. Price became your only invariable left to clear imbalances.[3]

China is intent on getting the resources needed to sustain its soaring economy, and it is taking its quest to lock down sources of oil and other necessary raw materials across the globe. With the Middle East mired in long-term instability, China has turned toward another major oil-producing region whose risks and challenges have caused it to be overlooked by much of the rest of the world: Africa. China's voracious demand for energy to feed its booming economy has led it to seek oil supplies from African countries, including Sudan, Chad, Nigeria, Angola, Algeria, Gabon, Equatorial Guinea, and the Republic of Congo.

It is not surprising that in 2004 global oil prices increased so dramatically. Everyone blamed China for the increase, but the Chinese argued that its demand for oil was only 1.3 million barrels a day, a fraction of America's 20.6 million barrels of oil a day for most of 2005.

---

[3] Lawrence Goldstein, interview with author, May 17, 2007. Goldstein is director of the Washington-based Energy Policy Research Foundation. He served as consultant to the Iraqi Coalition Provisional Authority in 2003 and 2004.

Now, says oil specialist Robert Ebel,[4] "the Chinese are wandering around the world trying to get equity in oil. The African countries couldn't be happier. China sends in one of its oil companies asking for access to an oil field and then adds: 'And, by the way if you need a loan for military equipment, we can do that.' They offer attractions that an international oil company cannot." China National Petroleum Corporation (CNPC) has invested more than $8 billion in Sudan's oil sector, including a 2005 investment in a 900-mile pipeline to the Red Sea; finalized the purchase of Petrokazakhstan (with assets of 11 oil fields) from Canada; and announced a plan to invest $18 billion in foreign oil and gas assets by 2020.

By January 2006, China had 18.3 billion barrels of proved oil reserves within its borders. To satisfy its voracious economy's demand, it has followed an aggressive policy of partnerships with other oil-producing countries. Some in the West have been concerned, but as Michael Elliot wrote in a *Time* magazine cover story on China,[4]

[o]n the optimistic view, then, China's rise to global prominence can be managed. . . . There need be no wars between China and the U.S., no catastrophes, no economic competition that gets out of hand. But in

China's State-Owned Oil Companies

Sinopec
PetroChina
China National Petroleum Company (CNPC)
Chinese National Offshore Oil Corporation (CNOOC)

---

[4] Interview with author, April 3, 2007. Ebel has held leadership positions in the CIA, Interior and Energy departments, as well as directed ENSERCH Corp. and the Washington Export Council. Ebel is an expert on energy policy, oil prices, and OPEC, among other areas.

[5] "China Takes on the World," *Times* magazine, January 11, 2007.

this century the relative power of the U.S. is going to decline, and that
of China is going to rise. That cake was baked long ago.

The less optimistic believe that the United States and China are
locked in a struggle over oil that will eventually worsen or lead to
violence. That seems like a remote possibility—but not so remote as
to be ignored. Senior military planners from the Pentagon—just in
case—decided to conduct an exercise.[6] The hypothetical scenario of
their "oil war game" was this:

- Iran initiated an attack on shipping in the Persian Gulf, thus pro-
  voking a massive U.S. response.
- China then attacked Taiwan.
- The United States was forced to split its forces so that it could reply
  to further military challenges.
- Venezuela then sent submarines into the Gulf of Mexico, joined
  forces with a Chinese submarine, and fired rockets at U.S. and
  Mexican oil facilities.
- The United Kingdom rushed to the aid of the United States and sent
  nuclear-attack submarines to sink the Venezuelan and Chinese forces.
- India sided with the United States.
- Russia remained neutral and did not participate.

To the media, the idea that the Chinese would send a submarine
halfway round the world and that Venezuela would declare war on the
United States were possibilities more suited to a Tom Clancy novel than
to a scenario seriously discussed in the war rooms of the major powers.
Still, the fact that the game was even staged gives an indication of how
dangerous the oil situation has become.

Indeed, as writer Vago Muradian[7] points out, the military calculations had three key interlinking elements, all related to oil:

---

[6] "The Common Thread Arising . . . ," Paul Rogers, *The United States vs. China: The
War for Oil*, China Institute, University of Alberta, June 15, 2006. The writing did
not indicate the date of the exercise.

[7] "U.S. Exercise Reflects Growing Tensions," *Defense News*, 29 May 2006.

1. Venezuela's perceived anti-Americanism,
2. Russia's greater political independence (stemming from its own oil wealth and expanding arms-export industry), and
3. Iran's putative pursuit of nuclear weapons programs financed through its status as the world's second-largest oil producer.

U.S. strategic thinking, contends Muradian, factors in these three elements along with nervousness "over the rapid rise of China's military power, and the country's zealous worldwide drive to lock down exclusive sources of oil supply." Heightening this "nervousness" were Chinese deals with Iran and Nigeria.

"When there's a lack of oxygen," observed oil analyst Larry Goldstein, "we all want the tank. . . . Oil has become valuable because it's perceived to be scarce. So the one thing the Chinese can't afford is not having access to oil."

In short, with little fanfare and no advance announcements, China has become a key oil player by virtue of its burgeoning middle class. Desperate to get its hands on oil imports, the Chinese have been more willing to take risks to compete with the United States. America wants to remain the dominant military force in the Gulf of Guinea; China requires closer political and economic ties with western African nations to gain access to oil and to counter potential U.S. penetration. China's competition with the United States over oil has had the Chinese running neck and neck with the United States. There has

2007 Oil Consumption (Millions of Barrels per Day)

World	82.2
United States	20.7
India	2.45
China	6.5

Source: All statistics from CIA World Factbook, June 14, 2007, except for India, where statistics are from Nationmaster.com.

A customer shops for audiovisual products in a Beijing department store, March 14, 2003. *Photo by Ricky Wong/Bloomberg News.*

been no similar competition regarding environmental concerns. China is simply not interested.

How do you get China and India to be green? As Robert Ebel queries:

> If China and India are to become oil players, how can you get them to pay attention to the environment, to commit on paper? We didn't ratify Kyoto[8] because China and India did not sign the agreement. As we watch the developing world consume more energy, as we watch China and India consuming more and polluting more, we have to ask: how do we get them to take concrete steps to reduce pollution?[9]

---

[8] The Kyoto Protocol, which was designed to reduce the amount of climate-changing greenhouse gases, was agreed to on December 11, 1997, and was added as a protocol to the U.N. Framework Convention on Climate Change. The protocol was adopted by its signatories on February 16, 2005.

[9] Interview with author, April 3, 2007.

In the 1990s, as Chinese demand for oil soared, Americans seemed to have little concern about such demand affecting their own interests. Their concern over oil seemed only to be about their increased international dependency on Middle Eastern oil and the possibility that supplies might be disrupted by terrorism.

China's increasing demand, however, has strongly influenced global oil prices. Until 2007–08, restricted supply caused oil prices to rise; now it is rising demand.

India's Economy

Even though its overall inflation rate is less volatile, India is concerned about inflation in its food prices. From 2006 to 2008, the price of wheat in India rose nearly 50 percent, and the price of rice rose more than 31 percent.[10]

India's economy is experiencing tremendous growth, with a resultant surge in oil demand—similar to what the Chinese had in the 1990s and early 2000s.[11] India as of 2007, was the world's fifth-largest oil consumer after the United States, China, Japan, and Russia. By 2005, oil accounted for 34 percent of India's energy consumption, but coal still provided more than half the nation's energy demand.

In 1990, Indians had to wait as long as five years for a phone or gas connection, but after the economic reforms a few years later, the country's entire outlook changed: global food and consumer-goods firms arrived on the scene, and plans were being made for shopping malls and movie multiplexes.

In 2005, India's economy had grown 8.7 percent over 2004. India's economy was expected to grow 7.75 percent in 2010. It had grown 6.7 percent in 2009 following the global turndown. The International

---

[10] "Can High Food Prices Win Votes?" *Times of India*, August 24, 2008. In comparison, U.S. inflation was more than 4 percent in 2007; U.S. milk prices rose 18 percent from 2007 to 2008, and egg prices rose 35 percent in the same period.

[11] India had always consumed less oil than China because China's economy was largely dependent on manufacturing, whereas India's depended on service.

A coffee shop in downtown Bangalore, India, Oct. 15, 2002—but it could just as easily be New York or Los Angeles. *Photo by Namas Bhojani/Bloomberg News.*

Energy Agency (IEA) predicted that future oil consumption would grow rapidly from 2.2 million barrels per day in 2003 to 2.8 million barrels per day in 2010. If the 2007 growth rate were to continue, then this figure would rise to more than 5 million barrels per day by 2030 (IEA figures).

For India, the foreign investment was welcome, but for that investment to work and for India to develop a middle-class, it needed oil. Although oil demand had grown by 6 percent a year[12] from 1980 to 2002 and 7.5 percent a year from 2002 to 2006, oil production in the same period had risen barely at all. While oil production rose 12.17 percent in 2008, it did not rise in 2009.

Because India's was the only Asian economy driven largely by domestic demand, its greatest weakness was always thought to be its inability to keep up with the Chinese manufacturing machine that produced the toys, clothes, and electronics that were flooding the international markets. The high cost of credit in India accounted for the poor state of its infrastructure. Even though it had a vibrant service sector, it needed a strong manufacturing sector and transportation infrastructure—both of which require oil. By 2030, said the IEA, India will need to import 90 percent of its oil.

The Middle-Class Indian Behind India's Oil Demand

The Internet edition of the newspaper *Dawn* ran an article in December 2005 explaining just who makes up the Indian middle class. It cited a twenty-eight-year-old marketing executive named Sharma Shaminder. She shops at a big, new shopping mall in an eastern suburb of New Delhi. She and her husband have a house, a car, and enough money to live quite comfortably. She is a consummate consumer who has little interest in saving money; as such, she is part of a wonderful new market for both multinational and domestic Indian retail companies. Shaminder and her husband are two of the millions of new upwardly mobile middle-class citizens in today's India.

Evidence of an emergent Indian middle class is in large part anecdotal (one estimate is that it has 250 million people) because only a small percentage of Indians pay income taxes or are registered as formally employed, but the National Council for Applied Economic

---

[12] More than three times the world average.

Research calculated that there were 56 million Indians in households earning $4,400 to $21,800 a year (the range defined as middle class in India). It is this group that bought 60 percent of the 800,000 new cars sold in India in 2004. In December 2005, it was estimated that another 220 million Indians living in households earning $2,000 to $4,400 a year could afford a television, a refrigerator, and even a motorbike. By 2010, India's middle class is projected to be 500 million, and its current $700 billion economy is projected to be more than $1 trillion.

In 2007, *India Today* reported that "[s]preading affluence, fancier retail outlets, availability of global brands, and a new disease called 'Techno-lust' combine to flood the Great Indian bazaar with the hottest products available. From the millionaire to the 250-million-strong middle class, everyone is indulging in retail therapy." With almost 350 million Indians younger than fourteen, the workforce will expand tremendously over the next decade, further increasing consumption rates.

India's quest for oil abroad has been ambitious. Indian oil officials have signed contracts for equity investments in all parts of the globe, not just in traditional sources in western Asia. In 2005, India spoke of a deal with Iran for a 2,600-kilometer-long gas pipeline through Pakistan, but as of 2008, that deal had not been signed. India also had signed a $2 billion contract for a 20 percent holding in Russia's Sakhalin-I field, from which it hoped to secure 1 million barrels of oil a day.

The West has only shrugged its shoulders at these efforts; its own risk-averse international oil companies had refused deals with certain countries, even when the oil was there for the grabbing. Although China had launched its economic boom from the top down and had its state companies execute its economic policies, India's boom came from the private sector's entrepreneurial and business groups.

Predictions for India's domestic market are bright. Its consumer class is expected to grow tenfold by 2025. Per capita income, at $1,000 in the early 2000s, was expected to triple by the late 2020s. Western investment is evident and growing. Foreign automakers— Ford, General Motors, Hyundai, and Suzuki—have opened plants

> The Indian economy is on the cusp of something big. . . . I am as enthusiastic about India as I was about China in the late 1990s.
>
> But the case for India is actually very different from the China story. What excites me most is the potential for an increasingly powerful internal consumption dynamic, an ingredient sorely missing in most other Asian development models. India's constraints, infrastructure, saving, foreign direct investment, and politics, are well known. Yet I see visible progress on most of those fronts. And the consumption potential—the organic basis of sustainable growth and development—is real.
>
> —Stephen Roach, chief economist, Morgan Stanley,
> *Wall Street Journal,* November 9, 2005

in India, and Korean electronics and white goods[13] are visible everywhere.

The effect on other oil producers around the world is not clear. The growth of oil demand from China and India seemed to signal that OPEC would reap the benefits of higher oil prices.

In the same *Wall Street Journal* article, mentioned above, Roach also noted that even though the Indian consumer was not yet a major force around the globe, the consumer sector's growth, however incremental, could drive market trends. He believes that India's robust growth rate stems from its heightening consumerism and that India's youthful population should also boost the Indian economy immensely.

In his talks with various firms in India, Roach heard plans for market and product development that focus on consumer-oriented growth strategies. Consolidation of the country's highly fragmented retail sector was expected once restrictions on foreign direct investment were lifted. India's 3 million retail outlets all seem to be gearing up for the competition they seem sure will come.

---

[13] White goods are major domestic appliances such as washing machines, stoves, and dishwashers.

The key word among government officials is *inclusion*—as India refocuses its development strategy to deal with India's rural poor. The inclusion effort has had its ups and downs, but political leaders express confidence that the new reforms will help dramatically in bringing many of the poor up to middle-class status.

Rural development would mean an increase in real incomes and consumer purchasing power. Small- and medium-size businesses are expected to be the main businesses to benefit from the reforms. As consumer purchasing increases, Indian GDP growth is expected to rise to approximately 7.5 percent. But what kind of pressure would overheated oil prices put on the economy as a whole?

AN INDIAN SOLUTION FOR RISING OIL PRICES

Having joined the ranks of world-class oil players, India has earned the right to suggest solutions for the global oil crisis. On one record-breaking day for oil prices, M. S. Srinivasan, India's oil secretary, had an unorthodox recommendation for cooling overheated prices: halt the trading of crude oil on commodity exchanges.

Srinivasan noted that, although there were neither supply constraints at that moment nor out-of-control demand, trading on exchanges such as the New York Mercantile Exchange (Nymex) was nevertheless contributing "enormously" to high prices. If crude could be eliminated from the commodities traded on Nymex, Srinivasan suggested, the world would "see a drastic reduction in the price."

Critics said that the oil secretary, in making the proposal, overlooked the fact that hedge funds, banks, and pension funds had poured capital into oil trading, taking huge risks, and gambling that demand would increase, and that these bets had become self-fulfilling prophecies, helping to push prices higher.

LET THEM EAT CAKE?

Unfortunately for the world's poor, expanding Chinese and Indian growth rates have had their impact not only on global oil prices and supply but also on global agriculture's product prices and supplies. As oil becomes scarce and its use damages the environment, many farmers around the world have switched from food crops to corn used to make ethanol, resulting in tightened food supplies, which in turn cause global food-price inflation. In August 2007, food prices in China jumped 18 percent, and in the spring of 2008, the Indian government announced that wholesale prices in the last week of March 2008 were 7.4 percent higher than in March 2007; it was the largest increase in forty months.

We complain that India and China do not have more of a social conscience regarding environmental policies and legislation, but we forget that the West, when it was first developing, was not so environmentally conscious either. India and China are in that stage of ramping up their development in which the West, when it was in the same place, was not so environmentally conscious either—and India and China have larger and poorer populations to feed than the West did.

CHAPTER 11

Power Shift

On December 4, 2007, a global conference was held at the Sofitel St. James Hotel in London. Attendees had come from Africa, Asia, and South America to attend the National Oil Companies Congress. They had been meeting annually since 2001, and they disagreed on just about every policy that might have unified them but one: driving the price of oil higher.

In 2008, state-owned national oil companies were responsible for most global oil production, especially in nations with large reserves, and they controlled about 80 percent of global liquid oil reserves. The major international oil companies (IOCs)—the so-called big five—control less than 5 percent of reserves. The balance of 15 percent is controlled by the so-called next 20 percent: the oil multinationals ranking just after the IOCs.

NOCs have an average reserve-to-production ratio of seventy-eight years. For IOCs, it is eleven years.[1] By 2047, 90 percent of all new oil supplies will come from developing countries.[2]

By the 1990s, as the industry consolidated, the Seven Sisters had been reduced to five. More startling was that the Sisters were now producing

---

[1] "Oil Sector's Big Five Face a Future Full of Question Marks," *Business Report,* June 25, 2008.

[2] International Energy Agency figures.

only about 10 percent of the world's oil and gas and holding just 3 percent of global oil and gas reserves.

The Sisters had ruled the oil world from the 1930s through the late 1960s. The Saudis and OPEC had ruled during the 1970s and the early 1980s (and the Saudis continued to lead the oil world through the 1990s and early 2000s), but catching up with the Saudis—and in some cases even surpassing them— were the new NOCs, whose balance sheets often exceeded those of the traditional oil enterprises.

When *Petroleum Intelligence Weekly* conducted a survey for its annual listing of the fifty largest and most important publicly traded oil companies in 2005, Saudi Aramco had maintained the No. 1 spot—because of significant ongoing investment in both upstream and downstream oil and gas operations. International oil companies and NOCs were even, with five each within the top ten.[3] Nine U.S. firms, seven Russian, and three U.K. firms were listed in the top fifty.

The survey looked at twenty-five state-owned and twenty-five privately owned companies that together accounted for 75 percent of global oil supply. The Western majors had remained the same or declined. The greatest gains had come from NOCs in Russia, China, and other emerging economies. It was clear that the balance was shifting from the oil majors to the NOCs.

In the face of rising global demand, although the majors experienced difficulties in oil discovery, the NOCs had been aggressive in oil production. Some of the national oil companies were acquiring skills of their own, while others had found workarounds to their lack of technology. They hired oil-service companies to provide the knowledge they lacked. This was a far different business model than partnerships with big oil.

A further factor was that the NOCs were supported by governments that could, if they had the temerity, alter the terms of contracts to suit themselves. Faced with that situation, the majors' choices

---

[3] The top ten companies were Saudi Aramco, ExxonMobil, NIOC (Iran), PDVSA (Venezuela), BP, Royal Dutch Shell (UK–Netherlands), PetroChina (China), Chevron (United States), Total (France), and Pemex (Mexico).

were few. They could either accept the new terms or pick up and leave the country, an outcome that seemed not to displease the NOCs.

Politics had also entered into the equation; fewer and fewer countries wanted to enter into deals with the essentially Western majors. With all the complaints the local population had against the West, signing a deal with a large U.S. oil firm could constitute political suicide for leaders of some developing countries. The first preference of these countries was to work closely with their own state-owned national oil companies. The second was to turn to the Russians or the Chinese.

The majors had two severe handicaps: the length of time it took to develop oil fields and the need to make long-term capital investments

Iranian President Mahmoud Ahmadinejad, right, greets Nigerian President Olusegun Obasanjo before the start of the Fifth Summit of the Developing Eight (D8) in Nusa Dua, Bali, Indonesia, Saturday, May 13, 2006. Rebel movements have been responsible for kidnappings of foreign oil workers in the delta region of Nigeria. In 2006, the kidnappings and attacks forced the Nigerian ventures of Shell Oil to shut down about 19 percent of daily output in Africa's top oil-producing nation. *Photo by Suzanne Plunkett/Bloomberg News.*

in unstable areas. In 1993, Exxon purchased drilling rights off Angola, but production did not start for another decade. It had already invested its new well-development budget through 2007, with nearly $50 billion invested in eighty projects. Even when it had a field up and running profitably, in situations involving terrorism or civil war, the major might be forced to close it quickly.

Governments controlled most of the world's oil, and teams from majors such as ExxonMobil were exploring and drilling alongside state-run companies, often in countries in Asia, Africa, and Latin America where official corruption, coups, and terrorism were a fact of life. When a government fell or when rebels took over a region, the majors had to move quickly. That is what happened in Indonesia's northern province of Aceh in 2001 when employees of a giant natural-gas field were attacked by local separatists who claimed a right to the province's gas revenues, and the employees had to be evacuated.

ExxonMobil extracted hundreds of millions of dollars' worth of natural gas in Aceh every year, but the field, in the middle of a conflict zone, was under siege. The Aceh fields subsequently reopened, but then Exxon had to confront human-rights groups that accused the company of supporting a repressive regime in Indonesia. Soon after the attacks, ExxonMobil was the object of a lawsuit filed on behalf of villagers who accused the company of turning a blind eye to the brutality of Indonesian soldiers who had been acting as a security force for the plant (the Indonesian military had a history of human-rights abuses). The company denied the accusation.

But the problems of the majors[4] are domestic as well. They are also being attacked by their own shareholder activists (although somewhat less violently than in the Aceh oil fields), who are demanding share buybacks and special dividends.

Nevertheless, all these circumstances notwithstanding, no one expects the Sisters to fall quickly. In 2008, ExxonMobil was still producing more oil than Iraq, and British Petroleum more oil than Kuwait and more gas than Saudi Arabia. Analysts who had been writing the

---

[4] The Sisters, in their amalgamated forms, plus some other large international companies.

A view of central Banda Aceh, Indonesia, on Dec. 10, 2006. Indonesians had a
30-year separatist war fueled by resentment that its oil and gas wealth hadn't
benefited locals. *Photo by Ng Swan Ti/Bloomberg News.*

majors off have seen earnings surprises to the upside time and again—
although the excess profits have mostly resulted from high oil prices
and high profit margins at the oil pumps.

What are the prospects for the majors renewing themselves through
additional oil discovery? Right now, not too good. There is disagree-
ment about why, but the major oil companies have not been making
major investments in oil field services and technology. The obvious
answer is that such investments are long-term investments, and there is
such uncertainty over the price of oil that the companies are reluctant
to invest in expensive technologies that will not be cost-efficient.

And what is the future of big oil? According to Kim Catechis, head
of Global Emerging Markets and Asian Equities, Scottish Widows
Investment Partnership: "Big Oil will be forced to break up and spin-off
valuable activities. This will appease investors, as it will release value,
but will inevitably result in smaller market capitalizations. Ultimately,
big oil will become little oil.

In fact, that is not strictly true. Big oil will remain big oil, but it will speak Chinese, Russian, and Portuguese. The valuation multiples of the emerging market oil companies will expand, as their superior fundamentals are recognized. These companies are the winners, as their reserve replacement ratios continue to expand, their future production growth is over 5 percent and their profitability increases. Big oil is dead. Long live big oil."[5]

The big change in the oil industry was the heightened number of companies that were from third world countries; it defied all the rules of economics and was a powerful indication of how a new definition was needed for the term *third world*. It had become all too clear to the

The World's Fifteen Largest Oil Companies, 2007[6]

1. Saudi Aramco (Saudi Arabia)[7]
2. NIOC (Iran)
3. ExxonMobil (United States)
4. British Petroleum (Great Britain)
5. Petróleos de Venezuela, S.A. (PDVSA) (Venezuela)
6. Royal Dutch Shell (Great Britain and Netherlands)
7. China National Petroleum Corporation (CNPC) (China)
8. ConocoPhillips (United States)
9. Chevron (United States)
10. Total (France)
11. Pemex (Mexico)
12. Gazprom (Russia)
13. Sonatrach (Algeria)
14. Kuwait Petroleum Corporation (Kuwait)
15. Petrobras (Brazil)

[5] "Is Time Running Out for Oil?" http://www. ftadviser.com, February 20, 2007.
[6] *Petroleum Intelligence Weekly* survey rankings.
[7] Strangely, Saudi Arabia's Aramco was usually thought of as a NOC, even though its origins meant that it did not really fit the profile of other NOCs

West that some third world countries and companies were powerful and competitive enough to take on Western institutions.

What made the rising strength of the NOCs even more impressive was the fact that the Sisters' revenues were bolstered as were integrated oil companies, selling not only oil and gas but also diesel and petrochemicals, which made their revenues much higher than those of the "Brothers."

It was the developing world's nationalism that had made the NOCs dominant, and it had begun back in 1960 with the formation of OPEC in Baghdad. That was the first time any group of countries had banded together to coordinate government policies toward oil and oil prices. It was also the first time that such individual countries had taken oil power unto themselves rather than rely on international oil companies to supply the resources and know-how in the quest for oil. In the past, because oil production was a knowledge- and capital-intensive industry, these individual countries had concentrated their national resources in a few firms or a single monopoly. A government would grant profits from mineral rights to a private company in exchange for the company's expertise and technology.

As oil-service companies emerged, they provided those technological skills on a contract basis, but did not demand a partnership stake in the oil resources. Now the NOCs had a choice between using the oil-field services firms or entering into joint ventures (JVs) with the oil majors, although the NOCs were now in a much better negotiating position. The NOCs began entering into joint ventures in which both parties would agree to create a new entity, contribute equity, and share in the revenues, expenses, and control of the organization. A JV could be formed for a single project or for an ongoing business relationship. In contrast to a "strategic alliance," a JV involved no equity stake from either participant and was a much less formal arrangement. There were many advantages for both parties; unfortunately, the JVs had a reputation of frequent failure or instability, particularly when demand was high and technology was in a state of flux.

One typical JV is that between PDVSA (Venezuela) and the state-run Belorusneft (Belarus) that was formed in December 2007 to explore for and develop oil and natural gas. The new joint venture will focus on fields in western Venezuela. PDVSA will control 60 percent of the company, and Belorusneft 40 percent. After Venezuelan leader Hugo Chávez's relations with some international oil companies worsened, he asked certain companies to accept minority stakes in the Orinoco with PDVSA in control. ExxonMobil and ConocoPhilips said no, thank you, and departed Venezuela. Others—Total, Statoil ASA, Chevron, and BP—chose to stay.

In the past, the Sisters decided on their own where to put their resources and where to drill. Now the situation is reversed. Rather than a handful of countries vying for the Sisters' attention, now a whole array of NOCs are seeking to form JVs with the majors.

India was one country that unsuccessfully tried to arrange joint ventures with the international oil companies. In the spring of 2008, however, India's luck appeared to be changing. Its effort at attaining energy security got a shot in the arm in April 2008 as its oil diplomacy began to pay off on more than one continent. In South America, India signed a deal that permitted it to participate in a joint venture to drill oil and gas in Venezuela, and Indian oil firms negotiated participation in oil projects in Turkmenistan in Central Asia. In another significant event, India boosted its effort to woo Africa's oil-rich states by hosting the first Indian–African summit.

In Venezuela, India's ONGC Videsh Limited, the overseas arm of the state-run Oil and Natural Gas Company (ONGC), signed an agreement with Venezuela's PDVSA to pump 232.38 million barrels of crude for a term of twenty-five years. India had engaged in some aggressive oil diplomacy. That India was now even able to compete for oil joint ventures was an indication that the IOCs had clearly been weakened.

Negotiating Better Terms

The NOCs, as they gained strength, began to obtain more positive terms in their deals with the Western majors. The choice for the private overseas companies was bleak: either accept new terms or leave the country. When the majors left, of course, the national oil companies acquired 100 percent control over their nation's oil fields and simply needed to subcontract out their oil-field services.

CASE IN POINT: SAUDI ARABIA

When ARAMCO was originally formed in the 1930s, the private firms continued to reap the vast majority of the venture's profits. It took until the 1970s for the Saudis, flush with their apparent victory in the oil embargo, to negotiate a 25 percent share of their oil revenues. By 1980, there was no more shared negotiation. The Saudis had 100 percent. The greatest NOC of all had pushed back the private majors.

From the 1950s to the 1970s, many Middle Eastern governments gained political independence from the colonial powers. In a show of their economic independence, several of them nationalized the assets that belonged to Western oil companies. (The Seven Sisters were simply sent packing, with compensation for their investment and technology determined solely by the host countries.)

It was a brave new world. By the early 2000s, the national oil companies, ARAMCO included, were way ahead of the majors in oil profits and oil reserves. Saudi Aramco had reserves equivalent to twenty times those of ExxonMobil, the largest private oil producer, but many of the NOCs (notable exceptions being Malaysia, Norway, and Brazil) still lacked the expertise of the private firms. They could complete the less-complicated parts of the drilling and exploration, but they could not fully tap the reserves. As a result, the world was getting less oil than it had when the monopolies ruled.

The Petrodictators

Many of the NOCs operated under governments that were dictatorships and had greedy and corrupt leaders. These leaders promised to use oil revenues in populist social-welfare causes, but usually the poor got little benefit and the leaders used the revenues to line their own pockets. Many of the NOCs behaved like international bullies; in fact, as petrodictators, they wielded a mighty global influence. It was because of some of them—principally Russia, Venezuela, Chad, Iran, and some of the other Middle Eastern states—that the oil world seemed far more tense and dangerous than it had in years.

One of the more powerful NOCs—other than Saudi Aramco—was China's CNPC; it had an 88 percent stake in PetroChina, operating in twenty countries. In some ways, the NOCs appeared to behave similarly to the international oil companies, pouring investment money into other countries' oil industries. CNPC had injected $8 billion into Sudan's burgeoning oil industry.

In other cases, NOCs—among them Petronas (Malaysia) and Petrobras (Brazil)—were competing with the majors in dispensing technology. Petrobras had developed advanced technology for extracting oil from extremely deep waters like those off the coast of Brazil; its technology development enabled Petrobras to compete with British Petroleum and ExxonMobil in Angola.

Malaysia's Petronas operated in Sudan, Burma, and twenty-four other countries; some 30 percent of its oil revenues came from abroad. Iran's national energy company, NIOC, had partnerships with Norwegian, Dutch, French, and Italian companies, as well as joint ventures with Chinese and Russian groups. By the end of 2006, British Petroleum and Shell no longer led the world's stock exchanges: Russia's national oil company (Gazprom) and China's CNOOC and PetroChina had pulled ahead. Only ExxonMobil appeared able to match the new Brothers on the exchanges.

Nevertheless, the NOCs were about $20 billion short of the funds they needed to extract the maximum amount of oil from their soil. They understood that the only way they could attract that kind of investment was to collaborate with one another, which is what the London conference was about.

Often, host governments were reluctant to let their national oil companies reinvest oil profits back into the industry, preferring instead to squander the profits on projects that were not productive for the oil industry or to reduce local poverty. Oil-rich countries such as Venezuela, Iran, and Iraq, sitting on the second largest oil reserves in the world, preferred exploiting the oil they produced and sold for their own self-aggrandizement rather than push their domestic oil industries to full capacity.

Venezuela's Hugo Chávez, for example, spent two-thirds of PDVSA's $7 billion budget on his social programs, which were intended to support his own political status. If the money had instead been earmarked for Venezuela's oil infrastructure, it would have returned more money in the long run. Chavéz's decision to turn PDVSA into his own political pawn has led to a decline in PDVSA's production capacity since 1999.

As a result of the Mexican government's decision to restrict foreign investment, Mexico's national oil company, Pemex, also showed a decline in oil production. Some analysts predicted that the quickly maturing and declining production of Mexico's Cantarell field would turn that country, the United States' third-largest oil supplier, into a net importer within ten years.

Because NIOC, Iran's NOC, kept gas at 40 cents per gallon for Iranian domestic consumers, it had been unable to increase its oil production or repair its refineries.

Russia, too, should have been investing in the upgrading of its ancient, leaky pipelines, but little of Gazprom's earnings went to that important pursuit.

In the late 1960s, it was hard to imagine that any of the NOCs' governments would challenge the major oil companies' industry supremacy, but in 1969, when Libya's Muamar Gaddafi came to power, that is exactly what he threatened to do.

Throughout the early and mid-1970s, OPEC members were nationalizing their oil industries, but no one thought that that national governments would one day be in a position to dictate prices. The shift of power from the Sisters to the Brothers had arisen from a revival of the kind of nationalism that began in Mexico in the 1930s and in the Middle East in the 1970s. It was only when oil prices dropped in the late 1980s and 1990s that the movement slowed; by the early 2000s, the shift

Nationalization of the Big Oil Companies: A Changing Tide

Iraq: Nationalized in 1972
Libya: Nationalized in 1973
Iran: Nationalized in 1973
Venezuela: Nationalized in 1975

in power to the Brothers and other national oil companies was very much in evidence.

In the early 2000s, international oil companies could not find new fields in the West, so they focused on oil fields in Asia. Located in the northern part of the Caspian Sea, Kazakhstan's Kashagan oil field was discovered in 2000. It was one of the largest discoveries of the modern oil era. Kashagan was owned by Eni with its partners ExxonMobil, Total, Shell, ConocoPhillips, Kazmunaigaz, and Impex. (A combination of physical obstacles and political interferences led to the postponement of production until 2012.)

In January 2004, the Russian government began making nationalistic noises. It declared that it expected to be paid $1 billion to issue a license for the exploration and development of one of the three Sakhalin oil and gas fields, the choice Kirinsky block. The demand for the high payment on the license effectively nullified a 1993 tender that had given ExxonMobil, ChevronTexaco, and Rosneft the same exploration rights. Having already invested $80 million in the project, ExxonMobil was especially taken aback. At the end of 2006, the Russian government took control of Shell's $20 billion natural-gas project on Sakhalin Island. In addition, the Russian government announced that Gazprom would play a leading role in developing the huge Arctic Shtokman gas field, which meant that the Sisters and their allied international oil companies would be relegated to service providers.

In 2006, Bolivia used its army to take control of several oil and gas fields. The Bolivians essentially held these fields hostage, waiting for private partners to agree to renegotiated deals.

In the past, when the Seven Sisters and national governments had not seen eye to eye on doing business together, the Sisters had pulled up stakes and shifted to North America and the North Sea, but those days were over. The chances of finding oil anywhere in the world had been so diminished that a Sister could not simply walk away because a country might renegotiate the terms of a contract.

In September 2007, Venezuela passed a law giving its national oil company, PDVSA, majority control of the Orinoco Belt's heavy oil fields, the largest such fields in the world. Venezuela secured $31 billion in revenues by using such tactics, but, not surprisingly, the move alienated several major European producers, including France's Total and Italy's Eni.

In the new reality, tensions were at the boiling point—but no one expected the pot to boil over in the near future. Leaders of the oil world, however large their reserves or however much they were making in oil profits, did not seem ready to go to war to protect their oil supplies. The Chinese were arming African countries in order to help them defend themselves and their oil supplies, but the Chinese seemed disinterested in rushing to the aid of an African nation that might be attacked by some revolutionary organization in an effort to gain access to oil.

In the summer of 1990, the Americans took on Iraq after it had invaded Kuwait, all the while denying that oil had anything to do with its rationale. The United States believed that, if it did not stop the Iraqis, in the very near future they would march on the largest oil supplies in the world—in Saudi Arabia.

The United States took on Iraq again, in March 2003, when it said it had intelligence that the Iraqis had weapons of mass destruction and just might use them. That Iraq held the second-largest pool of oil reserves in the world (after the Saudis), the Americans insisted, had nothing to do with the invasion.

"The only idea we have for the region," then-U.S. Secretary of Defense Donald Rumsfeld told an interviewer for the Arab television network Al Jazeera, "is that it not be producing weapons of mass destruction and it not be invading its neighbors and that it be peaceful." That was why, after the Iraqis burned their own oil fields in the opening hours of the war, Americans delicately danced around the question of rebuilding the oil fields; they feared that the rest of the world would immediately accuse them of seeking to take them over. President George W. Bush had spent little time trying to organize an Iraqi-led program to share the existing oil wealth; he was content simply to have the United States by default constitute the only source of protection and to keep the Iraqi oil fields from falling into the hands of Iran or Al Qaeda.

To some analysts on Wall Street and in Washington, D.C., it was obvious that oil was at the center of most ongoing international disputes. The potential for violence was becoming ever greater. On January 7, 2008, five Iranian fast boats raced aggressively toward three U.S. ships in international waters in a manner that was "unduly provocative" in the words of a U.S. naval fleet commander. The Iranian boats came within 500 yards of the American ships. During the incident, an Iranian voice broadcast to the Americans: "I am coming at you. You will explode in a couple of minutes."[8]

The prospect of an American–Iranian military engagement seemed likely: Both countries' ships were in the Straits of Hormuz, through which passed 28 percent of all world oil and where 55 percent of the world's crude oil reserves were held. In the end, the U.S. ships held their fire, noting that they were about to open up on the Iranians when the Iranians suddenly turned and headed back, ending the incident.

For several years before the marine confrontation, the United States had been seeking international support to force the Iranians to cease their nuclear weapons program; the United States had not succeeded. Cynics argued that the United States had merely been looking for a pretext to bomb the Iranians, with the idea of keeping American forces in Iran to "protect" its oil fields. If the Americans controlled Middle Eastern oil fields, then they could help ensure the stability of the oil world and hence the stability of oil prices, which was an overriding American goal.

U.S. Secretary of Defense Robert Gates said, "This is a very volatile area, and the risk of an incident escalating is real. It is a reminder that there is a very unpredictable government in Tehran."

Showing up in Jerusalem on a working visit a few days later, President George Bush was asked by a reporter why the United States had not reacted to the Iranian gambit. He implied that the United States would not act with such restraint if a similar incident recurred: "There will be serious consequences if they attack our ships, pure and simple. My advice to them is: don't do it."

---

[8] The incident immediately called to mind a previous incident in March 2007, when Iran had seized fifteen British sailors and marines in the Gulf and accused them of trespassing in Iranian waters. London maintained they were in Iraqi waters, but the Brits were nevertheless held for almost two weeks.

Wall Street was not pleased with the situation. Oil prices rose briefly on the news as traders weighed the seriousness of the threat to oil shipments along the critical shipping route. Before slipping back, oil futures jumped 49 cents to $98.40. The new breed of petrodictators was likely to create more incidents like this one as well as the Russian invasion of Georgia.

CHAPTER 12

Russia: Putin's War
Against the Oligarchs

In the fall of 2004, Russian President Vladimir Putin announced plans for a radical "overhaul" of his country's political system. The goal: to centralize power in the Kremlin. Putin had been opportunistic in using a hostage crisis in Beslan in which Chechen separatists killed hundreds of children. He argued that his power grab was motivated by Russia's need to win its own war on terrorism. The move was not the first time he deployed the power of the Russian state for his own purposes.

The handpicked successor of President Boris Yeltsin, Putin had been waging war with the "oligarchs," those businessmen who filled the power vacuum following the 1991 collapse of the Soviet Union and taken control of what had been state assets. The oligarchs had supported the government of Yeltsin until Russia was thrown into disarray by the collapse of the ruble in 1998.

Mikhail Khodorkovsky, president and major shareholder of the Russian oil group Yukos, was one of these so-called oligarchs. His net worth, according to Forbes, *was $15 billion. Because Khodorkovsky's brand of capitalism and his wealth directly challenged Putin's power, in 2003 Putin had Khodorkovsky arrested and thrown in jail on charges of fraud and tax evasion. The door was then open for the state-owned oil company Rosneft to win the bid for the remains of Yukos. Khodorkovsky has languished in prison ever since.*

137

A radical resettling of the flawed and unfair oligarchic ownership arrangements had been all but inevitable, but Putin's move
was equally flawed and unfair and was an indication of how the
central government or its thugs exert control over business in
general—whether foreign or domestic.

According to a Moscow Times review of more than thirty
cases, at least ten businesspeople were denied entry to Russia,
apparently for "national security reasons" from 2004 to 2006.
The expulsions appeared to be linked to business dealings,
and several businesspeople said they believed their Russian
rivals had bribed officials to blacklist them. If that was the
case, then foreign investors could have a new reason to exercise
caution when doing business in Russia. After Putin's invasion
of Georgia in August 2008, however, those same investors who
had flocked to Russia only a few years earlier—when Russia

Mikhail Khodorkovsky, once Russia's richest man and one of the so-called oligarchs,
was convicted by a Moscow court of corporate tax evasion and embezzlement in
a case that devastated OAO Yukos Oil Co. *Photo by Dmitry Beliakov/Bloomberg
News.*

had been the "R" in the BRIC¹ acronym—began leaving Russia.
It looked as if the story was about to become "Back to the
USSR." If so, it would not be a business-friendly place for
capitalists.

The current oil world has changed radically since the major oil
shocks of the 1970s. A whole new breed of states who can arguably
be called petroaggressors has come to the fore. Three of the biggest
and most visible are Russia, Iran, and Venezuela.

The petroaggressors had always been strident, flexing their muscles
inordinately, making threats, or delivering ultimatums to the West.
Starting in the 1990s and recurring in the early 2000s, however, the
new oil wealth pouring into their coffers gave them an even greater
capacity to throw their weight around.

During the Cold War years of 1945 to 1991, the Soviet Union wanted
to produce as much oil and gas as possible; as a dictatorship, it could
insist that certain client states in Eastern Europe and Central Asia
purchase its wares. It had an obligation to supply oil to the outlying
Soviet republics, but it was not interested in bargaining over price.

In 1917, Russia had produced 15 percent of the world's oil demand—
but its oil had never provided real wealth until the 1990s. Since then,
its stranglehold on some of the world's largest pools of discovered
and untapped oil had given it the power to become a petroaggressor.
In 2006, Russia became the world's second-largest oil exporter after
Saudi Arabia.

With the fall of the Soviet Union, many observers had had great
hopes that democracy would finally come to Russia. Those hopes
were extinguished when former KGB agent Vladimir Putin came to
power as president in 1999. One news story used the headline "Once
a KGB Thug, Always a KGB Thug."² There was no longer a KGB,
of course, but the new Russian intelligence agency that had taken its
place, the "FSB," seemed no different.

---

¹ Many exchange-traded funds were based on various Brazil, Russia, India, and
China (BRIC) indexes.
² Steve Watson, www.infowars.net, November 21, 2006.

At the start of Putin's presidency, the Russian economy was under-going a currency crisis, a legacy from the Yeltsin era. The government owed billions of dollars, the banking system was insolvent, equity investors had suffered great losses, and vast numbers of foreign companies had left Russia and gone back home. Public services did not function at full capacity because the government was not deriving sufficient tax revenues. As much as half of the Russian economy was black market.

Nevertheless, thanks to rising oil prices, Putin was able to pay off debts, increase hard currency reserves, and step up tax enforcement. In 2001, he imposed a flat 13 percent income tax. Although Putin had succeeded in bringing the country back from economic collapse, to continue on the course he had charted he needed Western technology to extract oil more cost effectively. For a while, it looked as if some relationships would be forged that would be advantageous to both the West and the new Russia. During the first six months of 2000, foreign investors began to be courted.

In May 2002, U.S. President George W. Bush visited Moscow and agreed to an "energy dialogue" with Putin. The two heads of state promised to reduce volatility and enhance predictability in the world's oil markets. Importing Russian oil, said Ian Bremmer, made sense to the United States, but somehow the two nations seemed unable to agree on terms. "The U.S.," said Bremmer, "talked about developing a strategic energy partnership with the Russians for years. . . . It's not gone anywhere. Part of the reason is that the U.S. is a consumer and the Russians are a producer, and therefore the Russians want prices high and the U.S. wants prices low."[3]

From the beginning, Putin seemed to have an interest in relationships with the West only when he thought they could be useful to him. In early 2002, direct foreign investment in the Russian oil industry was $4.5 billion, and most of that money went to high-risk, expensive projects in the Pacific Ocean and to building a pipeline that connected the Caspian oil fields to Black Sea ports. Russian–Western relationships were

---

[3] Ian Bremmer, interview with the author in New York, September 8, 2006. Bremmer is president of Eurasia Group, a strategy-minded think tank.

already showing signs of strain, but the honeymoon officially ended in October 2003, when the Russians began arresting Yukos executives.

Western oil investors were clearly confused over the direction Putin was taking. They wanted to do oil business but were shaken by an environment in which business executives were imprisoned. That said, they had been boxed out of oil investing in the Middle East and either did not have access to North American and northwest European oil fields or the oil fields were maturing and declining in production.

In 2004, Putin expedited approvals and set up duty-free industrial zones, offering investors joint ventures (JVs) with state-controlled firms. The JVs held out the potential for lucrative returns, but the Kremlin, not the private sector, had become the key decision maker for oil production, and governmental intrusiveness had dampened the enthusiasm of Western oil investors. ExxonMobil and the French oil firm Total declared that they would scale down involvement in Russia's oil markets. Between 2003 and 2004, capital flight from Russia increased by $9 billion to $12 billion from $2.9 billion.

Unwilling to rely on the Western oil technology and knowledge they had formerly had access to, the Russians were left to rely largely on their own. By 2005, Russia's oil and gas sectors were 20 percent of its gross national product and were generating more than 60 percent of its export revenue—30 percent of all foreign direct investment in the country. Unquestionably, as a result of the infusion of oil earnings, Russia's economy was back on its feet.

In 2006, Russia's real GNP grew by 6.7 percent, surpassing average growth rates in other industrialized countries and marking the country's seventh consecutive year of economic expansion. "Russia now has the ability to take it or leave it," observed Israeli scholar Mordechai Abir.[4] "They tell customers in Western Europe: 'We are now the ones with the whip. We can tell you: if we don't sell it to you, we can sell it to China, to Japan, sell it elsewhere.'"

---

[4] In 2007 interviews with the author. Abir is a fellow of the Jerusalem Center for Public Affairs and emeritus professor of Islamic and Middle Eastern Studies at the Hebrew University of Jerusalem who has specialized in Saudi Arabia and Middle Eastern oil.

Putin continued to display his oil muscle. In 2006, Royal Dutch Shell was the majority stakeholder[5] in the Sakhalin 2 project in Russia. Once completed, the project would be able to meet 8 percent of the world's liquefied natural gas demand. Shell had already seen costs double on the project, which was the largest integrated oil and natural gas scheme in the world—but the latest twist was that now the Russian authorities were seeking to repeal a 2003 feasibility study that had allowed the plan to go ahead in the first place. Because Russian gas giant Gazprom had been in talks for more than a year in an effort to take a stake in the project, it was not difficult to see which firm might stand to benefit if Shell's rights to the project were repealed. The deal was just another demonstration of the problems of working with governments that make up the rules as they go along to suit their own needs and ambitions. "That's why it's more important than ever," observed *MoneyWeek,* "that the West find sources of oil that don't involve relying on such countries."

In the fall of 2007, Putin challenged the $6 billion project of an energy-development consortium that was being run by American oil producer Chevron in Kazakhstan.[5] Chevron had hoped to double delivery capacity at the Caspian pipeline that ran from Kazakhstan to the Black Sea. The Russians had a 24 percent stake in Chevron's consortium but had long opposed the group's plans to double capacity from 700,000 barrels per day, saying that they were not receiving sufficient revenues. Finally, they decided to block the expansion of the pipeline.

"Russia," says oil analyst Michael Hiley,[6] "is the world's largest gas producer. They can be even bigger. Their pipeline infrastructure is terrible. Any time you get investment going in Russia, they have a problem where the Russian government takes over an oil company because they don't like the guy running it. There's political risk for those who are willing to invest in countries that have nationalized their oil companies."

---

[5] The consortium also included subsidiaries of Japan's Mitsui and Mitsubishi corporations.

[6] Michael Hiley, interview with author, April 7, 2007. Hiley is senior vice president and head of energy products at the energy company Fimat.

Russia's president, Vladimir Putin, left, stands with Dmitry Medvedev, Russia's first deputy prime minister, during a concert in Red Square, Moscow, March 2, 2008. *Photo by Yuri Gripas/Bloomberg News.*

Putin remains popular in Russia. He has his critics, but, although their words can sting, they pose little real threat to his rule. Gary Kasparov, the famous chess player and one-time presidential candidate, once said of him: "Putin isn't cowed. [He] wants to rule like Stalin but live like Abramovich[7]. . . . Putin's system is more like Mafia than democracy."

By 2007, Putin had brought production up to 10 million barrels a day. Russia effectively controlled access to the increased Central Asian nations' production, a situation that became clear when Lukoil declared that it would increase production from Kazakhstan 40 percent by 2010.

With 19 percent of Russian oil production and 18 percent of Russian oil, Lukoil was the dominant company in the Russian oil sector. From a global perspective, the company owned 1.3 percent of global oil reserves and controlled 2.3 percent of global oil production. In 2006, it had the largest trading volumes among foreign companies on the London Stock

---

[7] Roman Abramovich is a billionaire Russian oil trader who owns London's Chelsea soccer team.

Russia's State-Controlled Oil Companies[8]

Gazprom	Lukoil
Rosneft	Onako
Slavneft	Sibneft
Transneft	Russneft

Exchange. The model for Russia—state control of publicly traded oil companies—has managed to subvert capitalism to Putin's design.

The treasure chest of Russian oil was too irresistible a temptation for international oil companies. With a mix of stubbornness and optimism, those who had left Russia a few years earlier were back again with a vengeance in 2007, opening retail outlets, building auto assembly plants, and providing housing for a new and growing middle class. Russian initial public offerings floated, not in Moscow, but on the Frankfurt, London, and New York stock exchanges.

The Western majors had their ups and down with the Russians. According to oil strategist Ian Bremmer,[9] "BP does a lot of investment in Russia. First they got kicked out of a Sadamko deal, and then they got fined $900 million by the Kremlin. . . . It's a tough environment, but, at the end of the day, the oil companies are getting paid to come into these countries and pull resources out of the ground and the oil companies are providing a useful service."

Russia's Joint Venture with BP Corporation

In 2003, British oil company BP had entered into a fifty-fifty joint venture with a Russian partner. The venture, called TNK-BP, was headed on the BP side by executive Robert Dudley. Russia's intention was to bring BP's technology to boost output in some older oil fields and to

---

[8] This list is subject to change with mergers and acquisitions.

[9] September 8, 2006, interview with the author in New York.

explore new areas. The following year, 2004, as Russia had hoped, BP was indeed able to bring production at the older oil fields to 1.4 million from 1 million barrels a day. BP was looking forward to the fruits of its labor: new exploration and its booked proved reserves at Russia's Siberian oil basin.

Not so fast, said the Russian government. In July 2008, it lifted Dudley's work visa. BP Chairman Peter Sutherland said that BP was fighting a corporate takeover by its Russian partners that appeared to be backed by Russian authorities—just another nationalistic twist, shutting Western oil companies out of energy-rich areas.

BP has been pumping about 25 percent of its worldwide oil output in Russia. Many industry analysts predict that a company controlled by the Russian government, such as Gazprom or Rosneft, will eventually assume control of the joint venture, relegating BP to the role of minority partner—if it is lucky.

Russia's Invasion of Georgia: Oil Is the Heart of the Matter

In August 2008, Russia invaded Georgia. The reason given for the conflict was that Russia needed to keep peace between the independent state of Georgia and breakaway South Ossetian separatists. But oil, of course, is at the heart of the matter. Russia wanted control of the oil-rich Caspian region. Georgia had no energy resources of its own, but it is host to pipelines—built by international oil majors—that carried oil and gas from the Caspian region to Western markets.

The United States had backed an east–west energy corridor across Azerbaijan and Georgia to Turkey, which eroded Russia's stranglehold over supplies from one of the world's few remaining untapped oil provinces.

Russia had flexed its muscles once again. Neither NATO nor any single Western country acted to intervene.

CHAPTER 13

Iran: Arrogance as an Oil Strategy

In October 1971, the shah of Iran wanted to celebrate the two-thousand-five-hundredth anniversary of the Iranian monarchy. Next to the ruins of the ancient city of Persepolis was built a tent city comprising three huge royal tents and fifty-nine lesser ones arranged in a star-shaped design and covering 160 acres. French chefs from Maxim's of Paris served the gathered royalty and dignitaries breast of peacock on Ceraline Limoges plates and poured champagne into Baccarat crystal glasses. The contrast between the dazzling elegance of celebration and the misery of the nearby villages was so dramatic that the guests could not help but notice it. The bill for the party was $100 million. But "uneasy is the head that wears the crown," and the Shah's uneasiness had led to his imprisoning or torturing some 60,000 to 100,000 citizens.[1]

In January 1979, in the face of increasing opposition, the Shah was persuaded by Prime Minister Shapour Bakhtiar to leave the country. On the shah's departure, a seventy-eight-year-old religious leader who had been living in exile for fourteen years,[2] the Ayatollah Khomeini, returned to Iran. The Ayatollah, not willing to share power with Bakhtiar, led his supporters to seize power in a coup that came to be known as the Iranian Revolution.

---

[1] According to Amnesty International.

[2] In 1963, the shah had imprisoned the ayatollah for his opposition to reforms. In 1964, the ayatollah was released from prison and expelled from the country.

*On November 4, 1979, the U.S. embassy in Tehran was
overrun, its seventy employees taken captive. The hostage crisis
had begun; it would last 444 days.*

Although the three big petro-aggressors—Russia, Iran, and Venezuela— have all challenged larger and more powerful rival states,
there were nevertheless some variations. The most openly belligerent
nation has been Iran, which has declared its intention to build a nuclear
arsenal with the intent of destroying the state of Israel.[3] Iran also issued
not-so-subtle warnings to Israel and even the United States that they
should put aside any thoughts they might be entertaining about attacking
Iran because such a move could bring nuclear wrath down on them.[4]

The instability and uncertainty surrounding the Iranian Revolution
resulted in diminished oil output for the world and the highest oil prices
in post–World War II oil history. By November 1980, the combined
production of Iran and Iraq was a mere million barrels per day—
6.5 million barrels per day less than in 1979. But what was more
troubling for the country than the loss in revenues was the vulnerable
position in which Iran had been left. Saddam Hussein attacked Iran in
September 1980, beginning a war that would last eight years.

The double blow of the Iranian Revolution and the Iraq–Iran War
had led oil prices to more than double from $14 per barrel in 1978 to $35
per barrel in 1981. By 2006, Iran was producing 1.6 billion barrels of oil
a day, 5 percent of global production. Although it was OPEC's second-
largest producer after the Saudis, even a year later, in 2007, Iranian
oil production was only two-thirds the level reached under the shah—
about 1.5 million barrels below its peak before the Iraq–Iran War.

During the 1950s, in the spirit of its warm relationship with the shah,
the United States helped Iran to launch its original nuclear program as part
of the Atoms for Peace program. The United States and Western Europe

---

[3] "The European Union and Russia have joined condemnation of the Iranian president's public call for Israel to be 'wiped off the map.'" ("Iran leader's comments
attacked." BBC News, October 27, 2005, http://news.bbc.co.uk/2/hi/middle_east/
4378948.stm).

[4] The consensus is that the Iranians do not actually have nuclear capability yet, but
they are assumed to be very close to having it.

The Roots of Iranian Oil Nationalization

The Anglo-Persian Oil Company (APOC) was founded in 1908 following the discovery of a large oil field in Masjed Soleiman, Iran. APOC was renamed Anglo-Iranian Oil Company (AIOC) in 1935 and eventually became the British Petroleum Company (BP) in 1954, as one root of today's BP.

In November 1950, the ruler Mohammed Mossadegh nationalized the AIOC. On August 19, 1953, his government was ousted in a U.S.-sponsored coup in Iran and replaced with Mohammad Reza Shah Pahlavi.

continued to support the program until the 1979 Islamic revolution, when the shah was toppled and the U.S. relationship with Iran was altered.

Without the assistance of Western technology, the Iranian government temporarily ceased work on the program.

No less concerned about a possible conflict with the West than the global political powers were traders in the Iranian stock market and those using the Iranian bank system. Some $200 billion had left Iran to go to Dubai and the United Arab Emirates. In 2006, despite the country's strong oil earnings, the Iranian stock exchange, which had already suffered a double-digit drop in 2005, lost another 7.5 percent.

In February 2007, BBC News reported that the United States had contingency plans for air strikes on Iran that extended even beyond the country's nuclear sites and included its military infrastructure. Some speculation existed that such an attack might be prompted more by Iran's plan to create a euro-based oil exchange[5] than by a threatened disruption of oil supplies.

On the surface, the idea that creating an oil stock exchange could lead to an American military attack seemed absurd, but clearly there

---

[5] Before any oil exchange opened in the Persian Gulf, oil was traded only at the New York Mercantile Exchange (Nymex), International Petroleum Exchange (IPE) in London, and the Singapore Monetary Exchange.

were those in Washington who were alarmed that Iran might become the dominant center of Middle Eastern oil trade, especially if it were to switch to denominating oil prices in euros rather than in dollars. These observers feared the U.S. dollar would suffer. Information security analyst William R. Clark,[6] for one, predicted that if Iran threatened the hegemony of the U.S. dollar in the international oil market, then the White House would have no choice but to respond militarily.

But the stock exchange, known as the Kish Bourse, had already begun operations in February 2008, and similar oil exchanges operated in Dubai and Qatar. So far, they are trading only in petroleum-derivative products for the plastics and pharmaceutical industries, but Iranian oil minister Gholamhossein Nozari indicated that the second phase, direct trading in crude oil, would begin after existing operations demonstrated they could run smoothly.

To date, the Gulf states have not been quite ready to defy the United States and denominate oil trading in euros. For the moment at least, they are trading either in U.S. dollars or in local currencies, but they probably will trade in euros within the decade in Iran, Qatar, or Dubai.

Iran's goal for its new oil exchange would be not only to allow Tehran to use a euro-denominated international oil-trading mechanism for its international oil trades but also to try to establish its own pricing mechanism for oil trading (an oil "marker"). Since the spring of 2003, although Iran had insisted on payments in euros for its European and Asian/Asian Clearing Union exports, its oil pricing for trades was still dollar denominated. The idea would be to offer international buyers of oil the choice of purchasing a barrel of oil for, say, $50 on the Nymex or IPE, or buying it for, say, £37 pounds or 40 euros, on the Iranian stock exchange. The idea was greeted as a clear-cut encroachment on American dollar primacy in the international oil market.

The three traditional oil markers, or benchmarks,[7] that have long been used in the international oil-pricing system are now all dollar denominated. What was the big deal about which currency oil was quoted or

---

[6] Author of *Petrodollar Warfare: Oil, Iraq, and the Future of the Dollar*, Gabriola Island, BC, Canada: New Society Publishers, 2005.
[7] The three traditional benchmarks are West Texas Intermediate crude, Norway Brent crude, and UAE Dubai crude.

traded in? According to some oil experts, such a move could lead to a huge drop in value for the American currency, potentially putting the U.S. economy in its greatest crisis since the depression era of the 1930s.

Support for the Iranian oil exchange has already come from Venezuela, China, and India (the latter two have notably supported Iran's nuclear ambitions). Despite the fear of some analysts in the West, others have doubted that the new exchange would do great harm to the U.S. economy. After all, Iran's share of the international oil market had been only 5 percent.

Ray Carbone, a senior trader at the New York Mercantile Exchange, says an Iranian oil exchange is not viable. "They won't get enough customers. Very few will trade with them. They are under sanctions. The bigger concern is, if the dollar gets so low that, for other reasons, pricing becomes euro-based. That is not out of the question. It would not necessarily harm us, but it would be a low point for the U.S. dollar. . . . I don't know what that would do to the market."[8]

Few oil experts wanted to go out on a limb and say with certainty that it was oil and not Iran's nuclear program that was behind the American plan to attack Iran. Michael T. Klare, Five College Professor of Peace and World Security Studies at Hampshire College, says that

> I do not claim oil is the sole driving force behind the Bush administration's apparent determination to destroy Iranian military capabilities. No doubt there are many national security professionals in Washington who are worried about Iran's nuclear program, just as there were many professionals who were genuinely worried about Iraqi weapons capabilities.
>
> I respect this. But no war is ever prompted by one factor alone, and it is evident from the public record that many considerations, including oil, played a role in the administration's decision to invade Iraq. Likewise, it is reasonable to assume that many factors—again including oil—are playing a role in the decision-making now underway over a possible assault on Iran.[9]

---

[8] Interview with the author, May 3, 2008.
[9] "Oil, Geopolitics, and the Coming War with Iran," Michael T. Klare, TomDispatch.com, April 11, 2005.

Nevertheless, having had a taste of being a nuclear power, Iran resumed working on a project as soon as it could. By 2009, its first nuclear power plant, Bushehr I, was finally expected to be operational. The world did not stand idly by. Once aware of the reality and immediacy of the renewed threat, the U.N. Security Council demanded that Iran suspend all uranium enrichment–related and reprocessing activities by July 31, 2008. When Iran failed to meet the deadline, the Security Council imposed sanctions, blocking the import or export of sensitive nuclear materials and equipment and announcing that it would freeze the financial assets of any person or group that supported the program. The halt to those activities was to be verified by the International Atomic Energy Agency.

Threatened with sanctions, Iranian officials, though mindful of the risk, believed they would have no choice but to withhold their oil in retaliation. In March 2006, Interior Minister Mostafa Pourmohammadi was quoted by the official Islamic Republic News Agency as saying, "If [they] politicize our nuclear case, we will use any means." The conventional wisdom held that Iran would be unwise to use oil as a political weapon. A *Washington Post* headline called withholding oil "The Weapon Iran May Not Want to Use," but many observers did not doubt the country's willingness to take a hard-line oil stance.

The West had good reason to worry about Iran's nuclear program. In May 2006, President Mahmoud Ahmadinejad had turned down a European offer of incentives to give up uranium enrichment. "Do you think you are dealing with a four-year-old child, to whom you can give walnuts and chocolates and get gold from him?" Ahmadinejad asked the French government rhetorically, in a speech to thousands in central Iran.

The West was wedded to an oil-fueled lifestyle it would not easily relinquish, and tension rose—in global politics and in the oil-trading pits. Oil accounted for 85 percent of Iran's exports, and revenue from these oil exports made up 65 percent of government income. Who would blink first?

It was with mixed success that Iran carved out its role as a petro-aggressor. The mediocre performance of the country's oil program had weakened the government in its ambitions for hegemony over the Middle East, but it seemed as if its currency threat had been just as powerful as

President Mahmoud Ahmadinejad, of Iran, speaking during a news conference in New Delhi, India, on April 29, 2008. *Photo by Pankaj Nangia/Bloomberg News.*

its nuclear threat. Iranian leader Ahmadinejad had figured out how to make himself and his nation the most significant enemy the West had.

It seemed hard to imagine how, if Iran had been unable to maintain an oil program with twenty-first century technology, it could so quickly have developed a nuclear program. By all rights, the United States should not have been so fearful of Iran.

In a January 13, 2008 visit to Abu Dhabi, U.S. President George W. Bush accused the Iranians of threatening the security of the world. He further accused Iran of funding terrorist extremists, undermining stability in London, sending arms to the hard-line Taliban regime, and defying the United Nations by refusing to be open about its nuclear program.

True to historic precedent, Bush mentioned nothing about oil being at the center of the American dispute with Iran despite Iran's producing more oil than any other country in the world except Saudi Arabia or Canada. Any dispute or relationship with Iran would necessarily have to take that into account, whether the United States wanted to acknowledge it or not.[10]

---

[10] As of 2008, Iran had 138 billion barrels of proved oil reserves, nearly 10 percent of the world's total.

CHAPTER 14

Venezuela: The World According to Chávez

Since April 2004, Venezuelan officials, including President Hugo Chávez, have falsely claimed that the United States is planning to invade Venezuela in an operation supposedly entitled "Plan Balboa." President Chávez repeated this claim prominently in a September 16, 2005 interview on the ABC News program Nightline.

The allegation is false. "Plan Balboa" is a mischaracterization of a Spanish military exercise, called Operation Balboa, that took place in 2001.

Operation Balboa was a routine academic military exercise conducted by Spain's Higher School of the Armed Forces [from May 3 to 18], 2001. It included officers from different countries, including Venezuela. Neither the United States nor NATO participated in the exercise. . . .

The Operation Balboa documents[1] make it clear that the exercise was constructed around a fictitious scenario. For example, "United Nations Security Council Resolution 1580," dated March 21, 2001, is included. There was no United Nations Security Council resolution by that number in 2001; the highest-numbered resolution that year was 1386. The actual UNSCR 1580 was adopted on December 22, 2004, and pertained to the West African nation of Guinea-Bissau.

---

[1] Documents submitted by Yuri Pimentel, Minister of Communication and Information, Bolivarian Republic of Venezuela, and posted on the Web site www.vcrisis.com.

155

Moreover, all the Operation Balboa documents are in Spanish. The language of the U.S. government and U.S. armed forces is English. The only two official languages of NATO are English and French, according to NATO's official Web site.

Thus, it is clear that "Plan Balboa" is not a U.S. scheme to invade Venezuela, but a 2001 exercise by Spain's Higher School of the Armed Forces, in which neither the United States nor NATO were involved.

How did such a false story arise? General Melvin Lopez Hidalgo, then Secretary of Venezuela's National Defense Council, said in April 2004 that the "Plan Balboa" story arose after a Venezuelan Air Force officer training in Spain reported details of Operation Balboa to his superiors. In the May 2, 2004 issue of the pro-government Venezuelan weekly Quinto Dia, *General Lopez claimed, falsely, that "Operation Balboa" was a U.S./NATO war plan. Since then, pro-Venezuelan government media and Internet reports have repeated the story, and the government of Venezuela has continually mischaracterized what was a routine Spanish military exercise, in what appears to be a deliberate campaign of anti-U.S. disinformation.*

—Excerpt of letter issued on January 26, 2006
by the U.S. State Department

The date was July 5, 2005—Venezuelan Independence Day. Tanks rumbled down the main thoroughfare in Caracas as rifle-toting soldiers passed the official pavilion—"armed to the teeth," in the words of the country's leader.

Hugo Chávez, the president of a country that was a relatively small oil producer, had just accused the United States, the world's biggest oil consumer and Venezuela's biggest customer, of planning to invade his country. Chávez was having a fit of pique because the United States had sided with Mexico in an ongoing trade dispute with Venezuela and had expressed its displeasure over Venezuelan nationalizations of foreign oil companies.

Venezuelan president, Hugo Chávez, greets supporters on June 1, 2008, after an election meant to hold his fraying "revolutionary" movement together. *Photo by Susana Gonzalez/Bloomberg News.*

The political rift between Venezuela and Mexico related to the different visions the two countries had for a free-trade zone covering North and South America. Mexican President Vicente Fox wanted to establish a free-trade area stretching from Alaska to Patagonia. Chávez appeared to have aspirations of extending his brand beyond Venezuelan borders and sought to create a trade pact he called the "Bolivarian Alternative for the Americas."

Not only did the United States have strong bonds with Mexico but also it was uncomfortable with having an aggressive and hostile government so close to U.S. soil. It was hardly surprising that the United States would use its diplomatic rhetoric and influence to oppose such a government, and it had suited Chávez's purposes at the moment to portray himself as victim rather than as aggressor.

Hugo Chávez had reinvented himself as necessary throughout his career, but the pattern was usually the same. He would announce outrageous policies and take bold positions, and then when he realized he had overstepped and risked too much, he would retreat to a slightly more palatable position. He usually seemed to pull it all off without ever acknowledging he was responding to political pressure in changing his tactics.[2]

In what was a defining event for Venezuela's large reserves of tar sands, oil prices had collapsed to $10 per barrel in 1998 when Chávez first gained power; with oil at that price, the technology of extracting oil from the tar sands was no longer cost-efficient. If Chávez could not increase oil revenues and turn the economy around, then he risked losing his political base; his whole presidential campaign had been pitched to the poor.

Although some OPEC countries with a long-term view sought to keep the price of oil down and keep people from turning to alternative fuels or conservation, Venezuela, Russia, and Mexico wanted the quick "shot in the arm" that higher oil prices would provide. It was in Venezuela's interests, then, to violate OPEC's quota agreements, which it did with impunity. Russia and Mexico—not OPEC members but eager to expand their own oil industries—were also violating OPEC quota agreements, with the end result that OPEC had become weak and ineffectual. Chávez wanted a stronger and more united OPEC—but only if members were united in quotas that would allow prices that would support his tar-sands production. "OPEC must change and become a much stronger player in the geopolitical domain," he demanded. But OPEC Secretary General al-Badri insisted, "We are not using the oil we are selling to the world as a political weapon. We have not used [it] in the past, nor will we use it in the future."

There was such disarray that the time might have come for OPEC members' reunification—had not three events taken the decision about quotas and prices out of OPEC's hands altogether.

The first was the World Trade Center attacks in 2001, which caused oil prices to spike.

The second, on December 2, 2002, a little more than a year later, was a labor-union strike by nearly one-half of the employees of Petróleos de Venezuela, S.A. (PDVSA), Venezuela's state-owned oil company. They walked off the job in protest against the rule of President Chávez's

---

[2] "Timely Reversals Show Chávez's Political Instincts," Simon Romero, *International Herald Tribune,* June 10, 2008.

autocratic government and his treatment of oil-company managers. The strike brought the company's operations virtually to a halt for two and a half months. After the strike was over, PDVSA fired more than twelve thousand workers, draining the company of technical knowledge and expertise. According to oil watchers, the strike caused permanent damage to PDVSA's production capacity and remained the key factor in explaining continued subsequent declines in production. (Although Venezuela's actual level of oil production was difficult to determine, and the country and independent industry analysts offered conflicting estimates, most estimates still concluded that the country's production levels had not fully recovered from the strikes even in 2006, four years later.)

The third event was the U.S. invasion of Iraq in the spring of 2003.

By July 2005, oil prices had risen to $60 per barrel, higher even than Chávez's intended target of $50—straining the Saudis' goal of keeping prices low enough for people to continue their oil addiction and not turn to the use of agrifuels like ethanol.

The price was finally up, and, although Venezuela's production was still down from the residual effects of the strike, the sharp price rises of 2007–08 more than made up the difference. Chávez had not needed to concern himself with the politics of OPEC; the market had taken care of that.

Realistically, regardless of Chávez's and the United States' mutual threats, Venezuela is the United States' third-biggest foreign oil provider after Canada and Mexico. More than one-half of Venezuela's government revenues come from its oil exports, and 80 percent of the oil exports goes to the United States. It may not be a marriage made in heaven, but neither is it going to end in divorce. The U.S.–Venezuelan oil commerce will continue.

Chávez, says Larry Goldstein, president of the Petroleum Industry Research Foundation, is a pragmatist. Once the price was up, says Goldstein, "He was getting a lot of revenue into his system. He had the freedom to be what he always knew he was. And he could now stand up because he was building up coffers of millions of dollars. High oil prices

---

[3] "After Chávez Exhorts OPEC to Flex Political Muscle, Saudis Object," Steven Mufson, *Washington Post*, November 18, 2007.

didn't get him elected, but they have certainly helped him stay in power. And he's been spreading that around as he rubs the U.S.'s nose in it. He has relationships with China. He's exporting finished products to China."

Chávez represented the face of the new petroaggressor: he snubbed outside investors, therefore denying his country the benefits of the technology his country needed to bring his oil production up to full capacity, essentially shooting himself in the foot.

He distinguished himself from the rest of the crowd only by realizing that an oil superconsumer such as the United States needed Venezuela as much as Venezuela needed the United States. As the United States faced increasing difficulties in gaining access to oil, Venezuela was assuming greater importance as an oil source.

Chávez has seized majority ownership of $31 billion in American oil companies' projects, including those of ConocoPhillips, ExxonMobil, and Chevron. He has instructed Venezuela's military to prepare for guerrilla war if Washington tries to topple him, and he has purchased $3 billion worth of warplanes and weapons from Russia.

To some American oil analysts, although the idea was not palatable, it was certainly understandable for Chávez to want to renegotiate his contracts with the Western majors because the existing deals had been predicated on a barrel price of $20, not $60. As to who would blink first, although analysts were guessing the major oil companies' departure from Venezuela would not be fatal for Chávez (Chinese, Iranian, and other state-owned oil companies could take their place), few analysts imagined that PDVSA could sustain the oil-production levels that U.S. expertise had supported.

Chavéz was employing oil revenues for his social projects—a laudable-enough strategy—but at the expense of investing those oil revenues back into his oil infrastructure. What was more damaging to his cause was that he had created enough legal uncertainty to make countries such as Brazil and India reluctant to invest heavily in Venezuela.

Chávez, in the view of senior oil journalist Tom Wallin,[4] had a certain political sophistication, but he was more than likely going to damage his nation's economy.

---

[4] Interviews with the author, May 21, 2007 and November 29, 2007.

"There is a lot of domestic political wisdom in Chávez's policies," says Wallin. "You have a country with a huge impoverished majority who has aspired to becoming better off; they have been told all their lives: we're a rich country, we should have these benefits. Like a lot of oil countries, there's this huge wealth concentrated in a few hands. There's a desire for a redistribution of that oil wealth. From a political perspective, and seeing countries like that, it's a very understandable thing. It's a very human thing. From a domestic political standpoint he's making the right move to show that he's getting this stuff back in government hands, taking it away from the foreign companies, building hospitals and clinics and food stores, distributing it to the public.

"In terms of the economy and the future of the oil industry there, it's a big mistake. It's hard to see how they're going to be as prosperous and successful. The old economic and political model is clearly broken, but the new approach does not work well either. For example, it does not provide a new way to get the technology they need for the heavy oil in Venezuela.

"That gets back to the question of why they continue to sell all this oil to the U.S. They're going to be paying for that in the future in terms of how much it gets developed, how fast. They're talking about bringing in Chinese oil companies, but the Chinese don't have the capability or experience."

On May 1, 2007, a new Chávez-decreed law took effect that nationalized the last remaining oil-production sites under foreign-company

Name-Calling at the United Nations

In a speech on Sept. 19, 2006, President Chávez spoke at the United Nations, commenting on Mr. Bush's appearance before that body a day earlier: "The devil came here yesterday," said Chávez, referring to the U.S. president, and "It still smells of sulphur today," he added.

—BBC News, September 20, 2006

control. The nationalization affected oil production in the Orinoco Belt, which has the world's largest reserves of extra-heavy oil. Earlier arrangements had given PDVSA a minority stake. The previous joint ventures involved ExxonMobil, ChevronTexaco, Statoil, Conoco-Phillips, and BP, and were to be transformed so that PDVSA would have a minimum 60 percent stake.

Chávez stressed, though, that foreign oil companies were still welcome in Venezuela—just not as majority stakeholders. His government, Chávez said, did not want them to depart Venezuela, only to accept being minority partners. The owner of the joint ventures would have to be PDVSA, and the oil business would be in Venezuelan hands.

The investments at stake were large by any measure, ranging from $2.5 billion to $4.5 billion (what Conoco stood to lose if Venezuela took ownership of its heavy oil projects). Exxon stood to lose about $800 million.

In 2005, Chávez had signed oil agreements with Argentina, Brazil, and his Caribbean neighbors, and he had also sought to strengthen links with China through oil agreements. Chávez's forays around the world seemed designed to do battle, economically at least, with the United States. Thanks to higher oil prices, Chávez's newfound oil revenues gave him the clout to embark on a bold strategy aimed at fomenting conflict between the developing nations with great natural resources and the developed nations with great oil demands.

Among his own citizens, some feared Chávez would precipitate a conflict. Others applauded his strategy and accepted his argument that the developing world, with 85 percent of the world's oil reserves, could only benefit from the expected turbulence on the oil markets. Most American oil analysts believed that Chávez had done great harm to his country both economically and politically.

To Michael Hiley,[5] Venezuela was a perfect example of a country that had nationalized its oil companies and was now paying the price; the country was hard pressed to persuade foreign companies they needed to risk their capital or technology in Venezuela. "They can't even produce their quotas," says Hiley. "When there were

---

[5] Michael Hiley, interview with the author, April 7, 2007.

Freedom of Speech, Venezuelan Style

"Lying" is a federal crime, but . . .
only the government can determine what is a lie and what is truth.
There is no "censorship," but . . .
the president can suspend radio and television broadcasts if he
deems it "in the national interest."
There is "free speech," but . . .
"insulting" a government official is against the law.
"Social responsibility" of radio and television is endorsed, but . . .
continuous death threats are made against journalists.
"There is no censorship," say Chávez supporters, but . . .
the government effectively controls the media.

strikes in 2002, they shut down a lot of oil wells; they mostly haven't come back. . . . They don't have access to the world's capital to develop their assets properly. Nigeria is similar, but they at least have Chevron, and Shell in there. . . ."

What would the impact be on the United States if Venezuela were to carry out its threats not to supply oil to the United States?

"I don't think it matters," says Hiley, "because oil is a global commodity. Cargos for the right price will come to the U.S. from Australia. Stuff goes from the Mediterranean to Asia; it goes all over the globe; so, if we weren't going to buy Chávez's oil out of Venezuela, maybe we'll buy Mexican oil. Being a global commodity, unless every country in the world needs to buy Venezuelan oil—there's no effect."

As of October 2009, Venezuela's exports of oil and fuel to the United States were falling 17.9 percent from the previous October.

China and Venezuela signed agreements in December 2009 to help Venezuela develop possible oil sources. Venezuela's goal is to increase oil sales to China, making it less reliant on selling its oil to the United States.

CHAPTER 15

Brazil and Petrobras: A National Oil Company in a Better World

Between May 9 and June 8, 1992, Brazilian inflation was 22.94 percent, up from 22.53 percent in the previous four-week period, according to the Economic Research Institute of the University of São Paulo. That would be equivalent to an annual inflation rate of more than 1,300 percent.

In an attempt to control the inflation, the government set artificially low prices for Petrobras's[1] products, and Petrobras lost much-needed investment capital. While other oil companies saw windfall profits from the price increase in oil during the 1991 Gulf War, Petrobras was forced to sell high-priced imported oil at a loss. During those years, the joke was that Petrobras was such a laggard that it should change its name to "Petrosaurus." Petrobras workers were only 25 percent as productive as the industry average, and Brazil was forced to import almost half of its oil.

Astonishingly, by 2008, Brazil had become energy self-sufficient and a net exporter of oil. Today, Petrobras is Brazil's largest oil company and one of the fifty largest companies in the world— larger than Microsoft, AT&T, and Wal-Mart.

In 1953, when Petrobras was created, the nationalist rallying cry was "O petróleo é nosso!" ("The oil is ours!") The company was created as a result of the efforts of Brazil's fascist president Getulio Vargas, whose

---

[1] Petróleo Brasileiro SA.

165

hope was to develop a means of concentrating Brazilian petroleum in the hands of the state.

After Brazil's misfortunes with currency in the latter part of the twentieth century, it was Fernando Henrique Cardoso, who was elected president of Brazil in 1994, who helped turn the Brazilian economy around and, incidentally, transform Petrobras. Cardoso realized that Petrobras badly needed restructuring and began taking steps in that direction. When the powerful oil workers' union learned that Cardoso wanted to shake the company up, however, they went on strike. The strike backfired, becoming unpopular when Brazilian kitchens ran short of gas and Brazilian service stations forced citizens to endure long lines.

Cardoso might have been against privatization, but he did realize that market strategies like taking the company public[2] or competing with

How Brazil Became a Net Exporter of Oil

1. Brazil developed an ethanol made from sugar cane, which is proving to be a cost-effective alternative to gasoline. Brazilian drivers can now choose gasoline, diesel, ethanol, or natural gas to fuel their cars. In 2008, Brazil became energy independent and a net exporter of oil.

2. In 2007, Brazil discovered the Tupi oil field, a new deepwater field estimated to hold the equivalent of 5 billion to 8 billion barrels of light crude oil. The new oil, along with refining projects under way by Petrobras, could eventually make Brazil a larger exporter of gasoline, adding to supplies in the United States and certain other countries where it is all but impossible to build new refineries. Tupi is the world's biggest oil find since a 12-billion-barrel field was discovered in 2000 in Kazakhstan.

---

[2] The majority of Petrobras's common shares, with voting rights, are owned by the Brazilian government.

The Petrobras 54 offshore drilling platform stationed in Niteroi, Brazil, on August 21, 2007. *Photo by Pedro Lobo/Bloomberg News.*

international oil companies could be very useful, even for a national oil company. Cardoso's strategies paid off, and the government began permitting foreign operators to bid against Petrobras for offshore blocks in 1999. Petrobras owned oil refineries and oil tankers and became the world's leader in the development of advanced technology for deepwater and ultra-deepwater oil production.

By way of preparing Petrobras for the competition, Cardoso named an investment banker, Henri Philippe Reichstul, as president of the company. Reichstul straightened out questionable deals with suppliers, began an incentive-based bonus system for managers, acknowledged billions of dollars in pension and health liabilities, and cleaned up Petrobras's balance sheet. His management allowed Petrobras to develop as oil-producing countries elsewhere did, with prices comparable to those of foreign competitors. During the first six months of 2003, production at Petrobras increased at a rate of 10.7 percent year after year. By 2007, Petrobras had more crude reserves than Chevron and lower exploration costs than ExxonMobil. Today Petrobras controls major oil and power assets, as well as related business activities, in eighteen countries in Africa, North America, South America, Europe, and Asia. Its assets total $133.5 billion.

Petrobras is not only one of the world's biggest oil producers but also the world's biggest biofuel producer. On December 19, 2005, Petrobras announced a contract with the Japanese company Nippon Hanbai for the creation of a Japanese-based joint venture, called Brazil-Japan Ethanol, to import ethanol from Brazil. Petrobras thus became a major part of the Brazilian ethanol industry. Although President George Bush had set a goal that by 2005 he would replace three-fourths of the oil the United States imported from the Middle East with American ethanol, the goal had not yet been reached in 2008. Brazil not only is already satisfying half its domestic passenger-vehicle fuel demand with ethanol but also is exporting its biofuels to India, Venezuela, Nigeria, the United States, and other countries. The company is building the world's first major biofuel pipeline and has plans to spend $54 billion on its biofuel production and distribution facilities by fiscal year 2010.

Petrobras has hosted visitors from numerous countries, including Mexico, Nigeria, and Peru, who sought to emulate Brazil's energy model. Some countries' oil companies, such as Norway's state-controlled Statoil ASA, came seeking joint ventures in hopes of gaining access to both Brazil's reserves and Petrobras's technology. So important was this deal to Norway that King Harald V himself came to Rio in 2003 to formalize it.

In 2000, Brazil's government made an offering of a 16 percent[3] stake in Petrobras on exchanges in New York and São Paulo. Petrobras had already been trading in Brazil, but, when its offering was made in the United States, the impact on its governance was enormous: New York required far more transparency than did São Paulo. The additional transparency, however, did not hurt the company. Petrobras's shares are now among the most widely traded nondomestic shares on the New York Stock Exchange, with outside shareholders holding 60 percent of total equity. In addition, unlike some other national oil

---

[3] U.S. $4 billion.

companies (NOCs) that imposed few constraints on foreign companies hoping to do business with a national oil company, Brazil passed legislation on environmental and labor requirements for international operators.

In the early 2000s, Petrobras was expanding; the company paid $1 billion for 59 percent of Argentina's second-largest oil producer, Perez Companc (Pecom). By 2008, Petrobras was operating in twenty-seven countries, more than twice as many as a decade earlier.[4] Petrobras officials enjoyed the company's dual identity: the embodiment of Brazilian nationalism *and* a Wall Street growth play. Says Petrobras financial director Almir Guilherme Barbassa, "We view ourselves as having the best of both worlds."

Tadpoles and Technology

Petrobras has drawn on the best minds in the country from both its own research laboratories and its research arrangement with the country's universities. One such venture was a large water tank at the Federal University of Rio de Janeiro. The 50-foot-deep tank simulated winds and waves encountered offshore and ultimately helped in the design of safer platforms. Another venture is a robot that cleans the gunk out of offshore pipelines. The engineer who designed the robot had been inspired by his studies of the swimming motion of tadpoles.

Another example of Petrobras's innovation was that, instead of using a conventional steel anchor to moor its platforms, the company found it more efficient to send a 55-foot-long, 100-ton torpedo to the bottom of the ocean, where it embedded itself in the ocean floor while tethered to the rig by a high-strength polyester cord. This was for its Platform 37 in the Atlantic, which was a floating production unit made from a converted tanker.

---

[4] The company's international reputation for technological advances got a boost when it became the first oil company to win U.S. regulatory approval to deploy a floating platform in the Gulf of Mexico.

Jose Sergio Gabrielli, president and CEO of Petróleo Brasileiro SA, in Brasilia, Brazil, June 3, 2008. *Photo by Adriano Machado/Bloomberg News.*

In August 2009, hoping to exploit the world's most important oil discovery in years, deep-sea fields discovered in 2007, Brazil moved to step back from its decade of cooperation with foreign oil companies in order to control the extraction itself. International geologists estimate that the fields might hold tens of billion barrels of recoverable oil.

OUTSHINING THE COMPETITION

Between May 1997 and June 2006, Petrobras's value in the Brazilian stock market increased 1,200 percent, a figure almost as high as the country's inflation rate had been in 1992.

Although Petrobras contributes significantly to the NOCs' reputation as potentially the most powerful new set of oil producers, most NOCs have not been nearly so efficient at developing their oil reserves as the Brazilian company. At Venezuela's PDVSA, for example, production fell 25 percent after Hugo Chávez gained power and began diverting oil revenues to questionable social programs. Indonesia's state-run oil company, Pertamina, was so mired in graft and cronyism that it was forced to become a net oil importer instead of being a net oil exporter. Petrobras is a rare national oil company success story—one of a handful of NOCs that were outshining the international oil companies—a far cry from the NOCs of Russia, Iran, and Venezuela.

CHAPTER 16

After the Power Shift: Where Will It All Lead?

A major European nation invades a neighboring sovereign nation, absorbs it, bombs its citizens, and rolls its tanks in with impunity.

A Middle Eastern country's war boat within shooting distance of a U.S. vessel threatens to open fire in an international oil-shipping corridor.

Pirates off the coast of Somalia attack ships in the Suez shipping lanes, holding both crews and cargoes for ransom and forcing many shippers to use the longer and more costly route around the African cape.

A western African nation ruled by gangsters and thugs extorts money from the West as it reneges on its obligations to the World Bank.

Civil wars . . . killing . . . displacement of populations . . . inflationary food prices . . . corruption . . . human-rights violations . . . international extortion . . . property seizures . . .

Evidence of the changes wrought by the power shift abound, in ways both great and small. What will the new oil order mean for the world? Where will it all lead? Do we have any choices, or have we lost control of the situation?

The power shift means that the modern oil players have scrapped the old rules, and new ones are trying to seize power. The objectives of these new oil players are the same as those of the old: to make as much money as possible—but the difference is that the new players do not have a long-term view. Most of them probably will not survive for the long term. They want to hold onto the power they have seized for as long as they can and siphon money off against the day when somebody more powerful, more clever, or more barbaric will seize power from them. They have no thoughts of nation-building.

The power shift will lead to violence in the short term, as nation fights nation for the last dregs of a fossil fuel that will eventually be used up as surely as whale oil for lamps was used up more than a hundred years ago. It will lead to agricultural scarcities at the world's table as the "have" nations seek to take food from the "have-nots" and put it into their gas tanks.

The power shift will lead to an interim use of nonoil fossil fuels—coal and natural gas—and possibly to safer nuclear energy. It will lead to new, more ecofriendly and higher-tech energy alternatives in the long term, as people's wallets eventually dictate choices that their consciences have not. Solar, hydroelectric, wind, and as-yet-unimagined

Solar panels sit at Acciona SA's solar power station in Amareleja, Portugal, on Tuesday, April 14, 2009. The 46-megawatt facility has a production capacity of 93 million kilowatt-hours a year and is the world's biggest photovoltaic electricity plant. *Photo by Mario Proenca/Bloomberg News.*

sources of power will become more than experiments and actually offer solutions.

What had characterized the oil order of the past was its orderliness, its predictability, its accessibility, and its relative tranquility. In the past, a few companies or countries had ruled, and, although big oil or the Saudis and OPEC might have seemed dictatorial and monopolistic, they were at least businesspeople, not thugs. As businesspeople, they were as concerned about the future of their business as much as they were concerned about its present. They knew that stability was the basis of business, and so they had sought to maintain stability in supply and in price. In 2008, quite the opposite is true. It is instability that characterizes the new oil order.

The prevailing wisdom in the early part of 2010 was that control of international oil had passed to a variety of players. Often the Saudis were named, if only because they still produced the lion's share of global oil. But sometimes, one or another of the smaller oil producers or one of the big state-run oil companies was named—the so-called NOCs. Sometimes the perception was even that real control lay with the traders on the spot and futures markets.

The unpredictability of the situation makes for very nervous markets. One day, oil prices might be $150 per barrel; then on another day, they might fall back to $115, or $100, or $70. One day, experts might forecast an end to oil in ten years; and then on another day, a huge new oil field might be discovered and thoughts of depletion be pushed back again.

We are already using heavy oil, oil from tar sands, and shale oil reserves; the only caveat here is that the price of oil needs to remain high enough to make the heavy-oil refining process cost-efficient. More sobering is that, as high as the financial cost of extracting and refining

Percentage of Income Spent on Gasoline

In the first half of 2008, most Americans were spending 4 percent of their take-home income on gasoline. But in some areas, such as the Mississippi Delta, that figure rose above 13 percent.

these heavier or higher-sulfur fossil fuels may be, the cost to the environment is even higher. The market and the world seem finally to have grasped the idea that oil is a finite commodity. Whether oil producers can continue to produce it for another twenty, fifty, or one hundred years is irrelevant in the long run; consumers have become aware that oil alternatives must be found.[1] Five or ten years ago, many economists would have predicted that the global economy would collapse if oil ever hit $100 a barrel. When it did, rising oil prices finally made their impact felt. In March 2008, Americans drove 11 billion fewer miles than in March 2007, the first March decline since 1979 and the sharpest monthly drop ever recorded. A price drop followed, but it was reflective of the credit crisis and the recession rather than the supply/demand picture in the oil markets. Less global demand means a lower per-barrel price.

We have found Band-Aids for different cycles of the current situation, including, at one point, the temporary suspension by the U.S. Department of Energy (bowing to pressure from Congress) of a program to fill the nation's strategic oil stocks. But greater forces are increasing pressure on the federal government to search for oil within U.S. boundaries. For years, environmentalists had vetoed drilling for oil in Alaska, but now the idea no longer seems totally unlikely.

There are discussions of drilling for oil in the Arctic,[2] and there is even talk about what might lie below the polar icecap.[3] The United

---

[1] Oil players were given this lesson during the 1974 oil embargo. Had they begun to develop oil alternatives then, the world would not be in this fix today. Even if the price of oil drops dramatically today, those players will probably want to continue to pursue alternatives—for next time.

[2] It was not just the Americans who wanted to search for oil in the Arctic. In August 2007, the Russians placed their national flag on the seabed below the North Pole. A Gazprom spokesman said that the Russian energy giant expected major new discoveries of oil and gas reserves under the Arctic Ocean.

[3] Ironically, global warming, which is presumably caused by burning fossil fuels, has produced an unlikely benefit. In 2005, scientists found tantalizing hints of oil in seabed samples just two hundred miles from the North Pole. All told, one-quarter of the world's undiscovered oil and gas resources lies in the Arctic, according to the U.S. Geological Survey ("As Polar Ice Turns to Water, Dreams of Treasure Abound," Clifford Krauss, Steven Lee Myers, Andrew C. Revkin, and Simon Romero, October 10, 2005, New York Times).

States is building two new polar icebreakers "to protect its ongoing and emerging interests" in the Arctic and Antarctic, and Canada has ordered new naval patrol vessels to defend its sovereignty over the Arctic. After the Danes began drilling in Greenland, they too began seeking evidence to support their own claims in the North Pole region. Streams of international delegations from China, India, and Japan have been pouring into the Arctic region to assess their prospects.

In the last century, the world went through a trillion barrels of oil; another 1.2 trillion barrels were booked as reserves. If the current level of growth in demand were to continue, a trillion of those barrels would be exhausted in less than thirty years. Notwithstanding all the talk of alternative sources of energy, however, we are not in a position to replace oil—at least not yet.

The Search for Alternatives

Clearly, alternative sources of energy would alleviate many of the problems surrounding the difficulties of finding oil, but some alternatives do not deliver what they first promise. Ethanol is a case in point.

Originally advertised as a quick solution to America's dependence on oil imports, ethanol has now been blamed for driving up food prices, emitting more carbon dioxide than gasoline, and providing a third less energy per gallon than gasoline.

Even if oil companies were to meet federal requirements to use 36 billion gallons of ethanol by 2022—which some analysts maintain is impossible—that goal would still meet only 10 percent of America's current oil demand.

Because of oil, the world appears to be tilting toward more competition, more friction, more violence. Because of oil, China was wooing western Africa, Venezuela was entering into accords with Iran, and Russia had ambitions of regaining its lost power and glory. New alignments and alliances were being forged, and old ambitions being stoked—yet, with the dark cloud of economic recession looming, no one among the Western leaders has had the courage to declare an emergency. No one has been prepared to take the "Churchillian" stance of identifying

A coal miner emerges from a mine after a days' work in Liulin, Shanxi Province, China, on Tuesday, Aug. 28, 2007. Surging demand from power plants and steel mills in the world's fastest-growing major economy has helped coal prices rise five-fold since 2000. *Photo by Natalie Behring/Bloomberg News.*

the "enemy" and insisting that the citizenry march together toward an urgent solution.

When there is a major change in process or economics—a power shift—instability is a natural consequence of the transition. This case—of our moving from an oil-based energy policy to energy conservation and an alternative-energy policy—is no exception. We will continue to use oil—we have few other choices yet—but we will also use coal, natural gas, and nuclear energy. We will use hybrid vehicles, electric cars, our bikes, and our feet. The answer will not come in a revolution, but in evolution. The answer will be to decrease our use of foreign oil gradually, as we turn to more-plentiful and cleaner natural gas or, unhappily, to more-polluting coal and sour crude. And although we are making this gradual (but only stopgap) shift to reduce fuel consumption and to use alternative fossil fuels, we will have to work furiously behind the scenes for the real power shift—to domestic alternative-energy production—to free ourselves from oil dependence and to defend ourselves against the petroaggressors that have sprung up, like dragon's teeth, all over the world.

The new oil order is not so much an order as a set of moving parts in disarray. It is no longer a set of benign actors in a game that all have agreed to play in peace; it is much more a group of players who believe that the game is getting more out of hand with each passing day, but who are unwilling or unable to apply the brakes.

Demand will only get stronger. World population is expected to rise by 50 percent, to 9 billion, by sometime in the middle of the twenty-first century. The number of cars and trucks is likely to double in thirty years to more than 2 billion. The number of passenger jetliners is likely to double in twenty years to more than thirty-six thousand.

If, as is predicted, oil consumption is expected to double within twenty years, where will the tens of billions of extra barrels of oil come from every year?

The oil standbys—the major oil companies such as BP, Chevron, and ExxonMobil—have found it increasingly difficult to compete around the world. Fourteen of the world's top twenty oil companies are now state-owned giants, among them Saudi Aramco and Russia's Gazprom. Western oil companies have control of less than 10 percent of the world's oil and gas reserves. With costs of exploration growing, the veteran oil companies are finding it ever more difficult to locate new oil.

The Energy Information Administration's *International Petroleum Monthly* shows that world production for January 2008 was

Supply and Demand

- Oil output is in decline or flat in Mexico, Venezuela, the North Sea, and Russia.
- Oil demand could hit 99 million barrels per day by 2015, up from 87 million barrels per day in 2008.

—International Energy Agency

74,466,000 barrels per day, eclipsing the previous peak of May 2005 by 168,000 barrels per day.

In fact, in the years 2007 and 2008, although companies spent more than $100 billion in exploration, they actually found less new oil than the amount they pumped out of the ground in the same period.[4] What's more, the cost of finding new reserves in 2008 is now 200 to 300 percent higher than it was in 2003, and the size of the new wells discovered has fallen by about 65 percent[5] during the 2003–2008 period.

The early months of 2008 seemed to be a tipping point for Americans, who began to find that oil prices had become high enough to affect their lifestyles, and they were going to have to make some adjustments. By early summer, Americans in all walks of life began cutting back on gasoline consumption. Truckers pulled their rigs off the road to protest high diesel prices. Airlines began charging for blankets and pillows, items that had formerly been perks, and instituted charges for additional bags. Some small towns and community colleges switched to four-day workweeks to help employees cope with rising gas prices. Some corporations, such as Hewlett-Packard, increased their use of videoconferences, hoping to eliminate the majority of employee business trips. The use of company shuttles, carpools, and bicycles was encouraged. Even with the subsequent price drop, a longer-term trend is in place.

The power shift is gradually changing the way we live. We hear of populations moving from suburbs back into cities. We hear of hybrid fuel cars and smart cars. We see Vespas on city streets, solar panels on suburban rooftops, and wind farms in the country. We hear of people eschewing bottled water transported in transatlantic cargo ships for filtered tap water kept in the refrigerator. There are "buy local" campaigns to convince people to choose locally grown produce over that shipped from across the country or from elsewhere in the world. But the petroaggressors are only forcing us to take measures we should have undertaken ourselves. We can no longer say we had no warning.

---

[4] "World Oil Supply and Demand," *IEA Market Report,* September 10, 2008.
[5] Research compiled by Austock Securities.

As precipitously as oil prices rose in the early part of 2008, they began an equally dramatic fall by that summer. Prices hit an all-time high of $147.27 a barrel on July 11, 2008, and then began a steady decline so that by the end of the summer, oil fell to below $100 for the first time in seven months on September 15, 2008. Prices continued to fall and, on December 21, 2008, had dropped to $33.87 a barrel.

Oil did not rebound in early 2009, trading at about $40 a barrel through March and April. But by August 2009, prices began to rise again and returned to $70 a barrel, settling at around $80 a barrel in early 2010.

Despite this extreme volatility in price, the power shift that occurred in the oil world over the past few decades did not come to a halt or reverse its shift away from national oil companies to international oil companies. Too many forces have been set in motion, too many oil deals forged, too many new oil-wealthy countries have grabbed power and are unwilling to give it back.

List of Chapter
Opening Illustrations

Chapter 1. Edging Toward Violence and Chaos
A worker at the Sporyshevskoye oil field in Siberia checks the pressure on a wellhead cap, Tuesday, June 24, 2003. *Photo by Dmitry Beliakov/Bloomberg News.*

Chapter 2. Two African Oil Nations: A Study in Contrasts
The New Zealand Refining Company Ltd.'s Marsden Point facility, the country's only oil refinery, is pictured Friday, September 30, 2005. *Photo by Brendon O'Hagan/Bloomberg News.*

Chapter 3. China Invades Africa
A member of the Sudan Liberation Army, poses in Deribat village, Sudan, Friday, July 8, 2005. In Sudan's Darfur region, a two-year conflict has killed 180,000 people and driven 2 million from their homes. *Photo by Karl Maier/Bloomberg News.*

Chapter 4. Power in the Desert: The Gulf and the Middle East
The Dubai skyline stands behind an oil tanker being converted into a floating production storage offloading facility (FPSO), at Dubai Drydocks World (DDW), in Dubai, United Arab Emirates, on Wednesday, January 9, 2008. *Photo by Charles Crowell/Bloomberg News.*

Chapter 5. Testing the Oil System: The War, the Embargo, and Spare Capacity
An undated government photo of a technician working on one of the wellheads of the Strategic Petroleum Reserve. The U.S. may make loans

to refiners from the U.S. Strategic Petroleum Reserve to make up for supply disruptions caused by Hurricane Katrina. *Source: U.S. Department of Energy.*

Chapter 6. The History of Oil and the American Dream
Humpback whale tail slap. *Source: Shutterstock.*

Chapter 7. Ethics and Oil
An NRC Environmental Services worker cleans oil from Rodeo Beach in the Marin headlands of California, Friday, November 9, 2007. *Photo by Kimberly White/Bloomberg News.*

Chapter 8. Hedging: Insurance or Speculation?
Traders work in the crude oil options pit on the floor of the New York Mercantile Exchange in New York, U.S., on Monday, March 30, 2009. *Photo by Gino Domenico/Bloomberg News.*

Chapter 9. How Much Oil Is Left ... and How Much Is the U.S. Willing to Drill For?
Polar bears look for food along the coastline of Alaska in this undated handout photo. The species would be the first the U.S. has protected from global warming. Polar bears, the world's largest land predators, are losing habitat and access to food as sea ice melts. Further Arctic thawing might kill two-thirds of the animals by mid-century, the U.S. Geological Survey estimates. *Source: U.S. Fish and Wildlife Service via Bloomberg News. Photo by Steve Hillebrand..*

Chapter 10. Oil for the Lamps of China . . . and India
A crowd crosses a street in the business district of Hong Kong, China, on Wednesday, August 12, 2009. *Photo by Jerome Favre/Bloomberg News.*

Chapter 11. Power Shift
A view of Lampulo Port in Banda Aceh, Indonesia, on Sunday, December 10, 2006. *Photo by Ng Swan Ti/Bloomberg News.*

Chapter 12. Russia: Putin's War Against the Oligarchs
Pedestrians walk in the center of Moscow near an election poster showing Russian President Vladimir Putin and presidential candidate Dmitry Medvedev in Moscow, Russia, on Tuesday, February 26, 2008. The poster reads "Together we'll win. March 2nd, Presidential Elections." *Photo by Yuri Gripas/Bloomberg News.*

Chapter 13. Iran: Arrogance as an Oil Strategy
Mahmoud Ahmadinejad, Iran's president and a candidate in the upcoming presidential elections, gestures to his supporters during a campaign rally in Tehran, Iran, on Sunday, May 31, 2009. *Photo by Ramin Talaie/Bloomberg News.*

Chapter 14. Venezuela: The World According to Chávez
Hugo Chávez, Venezuela's president, salutes military commanders during a news conference at the Miraflores Palace in Caracas, Venezuela, on Wednesday, December 5, 2007. *Photo by Susana Gonzalez/Bloomberg News.*

Chapter 15. Brazil and Petrobras: A National Oil Company in a Better World
A security guard stands in front of the Petrobras 54 offshore drilling platform, in Niteroi, Brazil, August 21, 2007. *Photo by Pedro Lobo/Bloomberg News.*

Chapter 16. After the Power Shift: Where Will It All Lead?
Wind turbines stand at the Hasaki Wind Farm in Kamisu City, Ibaraki Prefecture, Japan, on Tuesday, July 7, 2009. *Photo by Tomohiro Ohsumi/Bloomberg News.*

About the Author

Robert Slater worked for UPI and *Time* magazine for many years in both the United States and the Middle East. He is the author of eighteen books about major business personalities, including *Soros: The Life, Times, and Trading Secrets of the World's Greatest Investor* (Chicago: Irwin Professional Publishing, 1996), which appeared on the *BusinessWeek* best-seller list; *Jack Welch and the GE Way: Management Insights and Leadership Secrets of the Legendary CEO* (New York: McGraw-Hill, 1998), which appeared on the *BusinessWeek* and *Wall Street Journal* best-seller lists; and *The Wal-Mart Decade: How a New Generation of Leaders Turned Sam Walton's Legacy into the World's #1 Company* (New York: Portfolio, 2003).

Slater holds a BA in political science from the University of Pennsylvania and an MS in international relations from the London School of Economics. He grew up in South Orange, New Jersey, and currently lives in Jerusalem.

Index